SELECTED POEMS

First published in 2009 by
The Dedalus Press
13 Moyclare Road
Baldoyle
Dublin 13
Ireland

www.dedaluspress.com

ISBN 978 1 906614 12 6 (paper)
ISBN 978 1 906614 13 3 (hardbound)

Dedalus Press titles are represented in North America
by Syracuse University Press, Inc., 621 Skytop Road,
Suite 110, Syracuse, New York 13244, and in the UK by
Central Books, 99 Wallis Road, London E9 5LN

Cover image (AN 00244330001) is 'Nebamun hunting in the
marshes', fragment of a scene from the tomb-chapel of Nebamun,
Thebes, Egypt, Late 18th Dynasty, around 1350 BC,
reproduced by permission of the British Museum.

The Dedalus Press receives financial assistance from
The Arts Council / An Chomhairle Ealaíon

SELECTED POEMS

Richard Tillinghast

With an Introduction by
Dennis O'Driscoll

DEDALUS PRESS
DUBLIN, IRELAND

OTHER BOOKS BY RICHARD TILLINGHAST

Poetry

Sleep Watch
The Knife and Other Poems
Sewanee in Ruins
Our Flag Was Still There
The Stonecutter's Hand
Today in the Café Trieste
Six Mile Mountain
The New Life
Sewanee Poems

Essays

Robert Lowell's Life and Work: Damaged Grandeur
Poetry and What Is Real
Finding Ireland:
A Poet's Introduction to Irish Literature and Culture

Translation

Dirty August: Selected Poems of Edip Cansever
(with Julia Clare Tillinghast)

As editor

A Visit to the Gallery
(poems about works of art)

to David Tillinghast

who saw more in the river than water

Contents

Introduction

DENNIS O'DRISCOLL

The day: Wednesday. The time: mid-Sixties. The place: a windowless room in the basement of Quincy House at Harvard. Around the weekly seminar table are intent young poets taking counsel from their straight-talking, chain-smoking mentor, then at the height of his fame: Robert Lowell. Among those students is Richard Tillinghast (a Southerner, born in Memphis in 1940), who—like his teacher—would find his future fate entwined unexpectedly with Ireland. Lowell lived, near the end of his life, in a wing of Castletown House, the palatial Palladian pile in County Kildare. How Lowell (1917-1977) briefly became an Irish resident is a tale as labyrinthine as the Kildare residence in which he once got hopelessly lost; how Ireland became Tillinghast's home—temporarily at first, permanently after his retirement in 2005 from the University of Michigan—is a less intricate one.

Tillinghast and his family rented a house in 'salt-stung, rain-washed' Kinvara ('at that time a quiet fishing village' of nine pubs and five hundred souls) for a year (1990-1991) on a travel grant from the Amy Lowell Trust: 'The grant was just enough to live on, and we gladly did without a television, a telephone, and a car.' His writing flourished there—many poems written, formal advances achieved, substantial critical essays (several on Irish writers) undertaken. No wonder Tillinghast began to increasingly associate Ireland with the writing life: 'With so much negative discussion of poetry in the United States, where it is periodically suggested that there are too many poets, that "no one reads poetry anymore", it has been tonic to live in a country where poetry enjoys a vital, secure place in the national culture.'

Even after returning to his teaching post in America, he gravitated back to Ireland for festival readings, summer reunions and trad sessions, Poets' House workshops. His singular voice became audible in Irish journals and newspapers; in 1997, *Today in the Café Trieste*, a selection of his poetry for Irish readers, was published by Salmon Poetry from its redolent Cliffs of Moher base. Since 2005, Tillinghast's own Irish base has been a mountainside haven 'at the end of an unmarked lane in a remote corner of Tipperary, three miles from the nearest stop sign'—a less dramatic location than Moher, but a no less beautiful one. Ireland too was where Tillinghast completed *Robert Lowell's Life and Work: Damaged Grandeur*, a critical memoir 'paying homage to the poet who taught me much of what I have learned about the art'.

Vocational commitment ('total dedication...tough-mindedness and perfectionism') and formal skill were the permanent lessons imparted by Lowell. 'A Lowell poem was not written but *built*', according to Tillinghast (who chose Lowell as the subject of his Harvard dissertation); and, while wearing its craftsmanship lightly, as it were, even the most casual-seeming Tillinghast poem—a few winter 'sketches' or an inventory of early morning scenes—will prove sturdily constructed on firm foundations. Although he had been steeped in the counterculture of the sixties, Tillinghast—who, in 1970, made the mandatory pilgrimage to Nepal, Afghanistan, India and Pakistan (where he lived in a Sufi *khankah*), and would later teach a popular Beat Generation course at the University of Michigan—has always written with schooled intelligence, consummate craft, and a deep respect for tradition. In 'The Button', an *ars poetica*, a dangling button—an 'errant discus of bone'—is secured on a jacket 'already a size too loose': '[I] put the jacket on again, / drew together the two halves of my person, / fastened that essential button, / and walked off into what awaited.' Yeats's 'stitching and unstitching' that seems 'a moment's thought', rather than the 'first thought, best thought' impulse of the Beats, is this well-accoutred poet's style.

While embracing the 'raw' freedoms pioneered by Walt Whitman and the Beats, Tillinghast never quite relinquished the 'cooked' aesthetic exemplified by his Southern literary forebears (John Crowe Ransom and Robert Penn Warren not least); it could be said of him, as he observed cogently of Lowell: his writing is 'more visceral than the cooked, more articulate than the raw'. Moreover, some of the powerful poems he composed in Kinvara, not far—as the wild swan flies—from Coole Park and Thoor Ballylee, display Yeatsian affinities of stanza shape and structure. An intimate sense of community—both in poetry and in society at large—was among the qualities which initially endeared Ireland to Tillinghast; and 'The Winter Funerals' is a poignant paean to neighbourliness, deploying eight-line stanza forms that would have earned an approving nod of recognition from his spectral neighbour in his 'ancient tower' at Ballylee:

We've brushed our black clothes off and put them away.
Someone is cooking, someone's out tending the stock
In the grainy drizzle that settles the turf smoke.
Obscured up there in the weathered sky,
The wind that troubled our winter still blows above
The village. We drink it at night with our whiskey
And stir it into our morning tea,
Hearing the tune Charlie played over Maggie's grave.

Only rarely does Tillinghast bring Lowell's midcentury domesticity to mind. The reader of 'And now I am home again. / I can sit out in my pyjama bottoms', for instance, may momentarily think 'Only teaching on Tuesdays, book-worming / in pyjamas fresh from the washer each morning', before being transported elsewhere by the Tillinghast poem. But readers of his celebratory poems of family life and domestic pleasure—subtle successes like 'House With Children', 'Rain' ('all of us in that long house together...house-partying on a rainy weekend') and

'Arrival'—will not think 'confessional'. Tillinghast's adroitness and tact with subject-matter allow for writing that is too nuanced to require shock tactics, and is all the more touching and convincing in consequence:

> Sure, we could have made a
> > more elegant appearance—
> I could even have shaved off my road-stubble.
> Yet here we were
> > emerging from the tunnel of distance, a family.
> Somehow you had entrusted your future
> > to my hands on the wheel and my foot on the gas,
> my skill with a screwdriver and socket-wrench and
> > fountain pen,
> my blood in the veins of your babies.

A lifelong explorer of other cultures, Tillinghast—enquiring and adventurous by nature—runs no risk of the solipsism of the confessional mindset: 'Travel is one way among many to get out of oneself—a geographical metaphor for psychic adventure.' Repeated visits to Turkey have yielded some particularly fine poems: 'Table' and 'Pasha's Daughter, 1918'. Signature tune of Tillinghast readings, at which it is often his opening poem, 'Table' (translated from Edip Cansever's Turkish original) presents a man who puts not only his cards on the table but his knowledge, experience and emotion too; the table that can accommodate the full heft of a life is itself the ultimate poem: 'Now that's what I call a table! / It didn't complain at all about the load. / It wobbled once or twice, then stood firm. / The man kept piling things on.' 'Table' is hewn in the same grain, and from the same board, as Marina Tsvetaeva's 'Desk': 'My loaded writing mule. / Your tough legs have endured / the weight of all my dreams, and / burdens of piled-up thoughts.' Threaded with silver and rifted with marble, 'Pasha's Daughter, 1918', recapturing the last gasps of the Ottoman era, finds Tillinghast in vividly sumptuous flow:

A Jerusalem cypress in her garden
That arrows the sky as a minaret does—
Its lines liquid as a page of Persian—
A leaded mosque-dome full and silvery in the pause
Between showers...

Although Tillinghast is drawn (as in 'Pasha's Daughter, 1918') to history more than politics, 'Ars Poetica', composed in the wake of the September 11 attacks on the World Trade Center, shows how persuasive he can be in public mode. This trenchant poem turns variously moving and scathing as its stanzas veer between contrasting locales and lives, tracking a camel driver en route to Khandahar as a B52 bomber zips above him, then inveighing against the America of 'NASDAQ, smiley faces, CEOs, / television, and Global Positioning Systems / guiding democracy bombs / into wars where people on the ground / shelter in tarpaper / shacks under roofs of corrugated tin'. It is not to the body politic but—as befits an *ars poetica*—to the body poetic that the speaker looks for redemption; to the private realm conjured from 'human fingers':

Revive me now
with anything low-tech, homemade,
handwoven from living fibres,
written with a fountain pen.

In that poem, as impressively elsewhere too, Tillinghast's tonal control derives from his preference for—in his own words—letting 'images carry much of the meaning'. He is absolutely not the kind of poet who lays down the ideological law, peddles a party line, or instructs readers what to think. His humane work attests to a conviction that, in a world which 'is everything that is the case', diversities and disparities which seem beyond reconciliation or resolution are not beyond our imaginative reach or empathetic grasp—an eirenic conviction conveyed with gusto in the rapid-action 'The World Is':

The world is a ton of bricks, a busy signal,
your contempt for my small talk.
It's the crispy lace that hardens
around the egg you fry each morning
sunny side up...
The world is a cortege of limousines,
an old man edging the grass from around a stone.
The world is 'Ulster Says No!', the world is reliable
sources, a loud bang and shattered glass raining down
on shoppers.

More outward-looking and international-minded though he is
than most contemporary American poets, Tillinghast nonetheless
registers his country's history on his pulse. His earliest childhood
memories (recorded in 'Our Flag Was Still There') include fleets of
images—destroyers and submarines, helmets and medals—from
the Second World War. And he is a veteran of civil rights protests at
the University of the South in Sewanee (where he was an
undergraduate) and peace rallies in Berkeley (where he taught in the
1960s). Above all, he is a Southerner, deeply imprinted with a
distinctive culture that was largely denied the comprehension—let
alone the appreciation—of his Yankee coevals, whose broad-brush
dismissal of Southern bigotry and red-neckery painted all white
Southerners in the most negative and conservative colours.

While by no means insensible to the more deplorable aspects of
Southern history (he no longer hangs a Confederate flag in his
study), his intimacy with the facts allows Tillinghast to remain
proud of the best features of his inheritance and even to joke about
some comically caricatural perceptions of it:

Southern writers are sometimes asked to explain
something called 'the sense of place'. This quasi-mystical
sense is transmitted at birth—so I am told—to every
writer from the Faulkner Belt, moist with mother's milk
and holy water, like that other supposed birthright, the
ability to tell a good story. If I had a dollar for every time

I have been asked why Southerners possess the narrative gift, I could quit my job in the North and retire to that mythic homestead, the Family Plantation. I have stashed the deed to it in the same attic trunk where I keep my Confederate money.

An ironist, not a caricaturist, Tillinghast is struck by how indifferently his generation regarded the heroism of its elders. Those who wielded welding torches in wartime shipyards and aircraft factories, or who guided the resultant vessels and planes to allied victory, are flashed forward for a preview of the poet's own contemporaries who 'in twenty-five years / stood baffled on the 4th of July among uncles, / drove good German cars, / floated in tubs of hot, redwood-scented water with friends, / and greeted each other with the word, "Peace"'.

Generation gaps are similarly probed in 'Sewanee in Ruins', an outstanding poem which finds Tillinghast's historical vision at its most panoramic and his human sympathies at their most acute. Fresh from a visit to the civil war graveyard 'where the past is buried under stone', his mind is focussed on the Confederate fighters who, 'possessed by a fatal romanticism', died as mere boys in 1865 when 'everything burned / but the brick chimneys / and a way of talking'. For his affluent, hedonistic students, however ('My pleasant-faced freshmen / from South Carolina, Texas, Kentucky, Alabama'), 'the Great War of the [Eighteen] Sixties' / is like some football game we lost':

> Not to ride and kill with Forrest all across Tennessee
> or die with Jackson at Chancellorsville
> or Polk at Piney Mount,
> or come back from war
> with health and nerves and worldly goods destroyed.
> The privilege of being young,
> the luxury of ignoring history—
> this is what their great-great-grandfathers fought for,
> though they lost.

Tillinghast may not have had the fabled plantation upbringing, but his childhood home on Memphis's South Cox Street had been in the family since 1890. He has written eloquently and evocatively of architecture, from the white clapboard of his native South to the Georgian townhouses of Dublin's squares ('as simple and perfect a design idea as the nail, the pencil, or the hammock'). 'Sewanee in Ruins' draws music from stone, coaxing forth the 'frozen music' with which Friedrich von Schelling identified architecture: 'The Romantics were right. / Gothic buildings are best seen in ruins: / sky-sprung clerestories in wild brambles, / Romanesque arches reconstructed by the mind.' 'Father in October' recalls life beneath the 'airy ceilings' of the Cox Street dwelling, including the constant maintenance work the building demanded of Tillinghast's devoted father, an engineer by profession: 'To marry my mother, my father found / In 1932, was to husband her house.' The poem's final line contains a tenderly ambiguous reference to the 'mortal house I judged him master of'. A wistfully beautiful early poem, 'Things Past', attributes a local habitation and an address to the locus of its recollections: 1632 Walnut Street, bathed in the 'bright fluid / time' of cherished memories; leaf shadows, sun circles, cookery smells, guitar solos.

Tillinghast's Irish essays touch on the desperate struggles of straitened Anglo-Irish families to preserve their equivalents of the family plantation, noting that their 'country-house culture' - 'molded in the age of Gandon and Swift and Burke'—'retained in its architecture and literary style the clean lines of classicism'. Writing from what he terms 'the insider-outsider vantage-point of an American who now makes his home in this country [Ireland]', there is clearly some identification in his mind between the plantation house and the 'house of the planter'. In the books of Elizabeth Bowen and Somerville and Ross, he finds 'consciousness of decline and ruination, as in the literature of the American South'. Romantic though a ruined building may look, Tillinghast—whether in prose ('meditating' on Yeats's Coole Park poems, for instance) or in poetry (set anywhere from his native Tennessee to George MacBeth's Tuam)—shares Yeats's proposition, as paraphrased by Ezra Pound, that 'the crumbling of a fine house / profits no one'.

Editor of a verse anthology called *A Visit to the Gallery*, Tillinghast—with his keen eye for architecture and painting (he took 'Saturday, summer, and sometimes evening classes' at Memphis Academy of Art)—can be a visually arresting poet. Among the most captivating images in his sketchbook are those of a bullfinch ('His honed beak businesslike, his burgher's / Stout midsection splendid, he perches / And preens his pink waistcoat'), cabbages ('each rubbery jacket bull's-eyed / like cigarette burns on an unfortunate table, / where slugs had tried to burrow in'), and a clematis ('Burgundy velvet like the robe of a grand vizier, / the clematis blossoms like big sagging stars').

In sinewy lines and solid stanzas—fruits of a lifetime's devotion to the craft—Tillinghast's most recent poems, undoubtedly his finest to date, fuse a sobering sense of mortality with the exhilaration of renewal, indeed rejuvenation, through love. 'They Gambled for Your Clothes', 'First It Is Taken Away from Me' and 'As Long As I Have These Saddlebags' share a vulnerability, fluidity and openness to experience, as well as a tantalising open-endedness in the writing itself. All roads in 'How To Get There' lead to the point of departure: 'Before decades, before skies, before the first summer, / before any knowledge of roads and weather. / Back to where you are an infant again, open-mouthed, / and the whole world lies in wait for your wondering eyes'. Refreshment of vision and restoration of potential, fostering 'deeper communion', are witnessed also in 'How the Day Began': 'What country were we in? Who was God? I couldn't remember. / The air smelled of everything.'

'In the Parking Lot of the Muffler Shop'—a poem providing a quirky context for Tillinghast's risky, but rewarding, willingness to inhabit everywhere and nowhere—becomes an improvisatory essay in everything and nothing, a divagating dalliance with the 'in-between' that playfully adopts a Heaneyesque oracular tone at one point:

I sit in the shade of this reservation
between a white Cadillac and a red pine,
and a voice says to me:
Archaeologise the ordinary.
Sing songs about the late Machine Age.
Chronicle the in-between.

Several of his lyrics of love, time and place—including the already-mentioned 'Rain' and 'Things Past'—are accompanied by the water music of falling rain, which acts as a lubricant of memory. 'What was it I wonder? / in my favourite weather [ ] in the driving rain / that drew me like a living hand', he asks in the opening lines of 'The Knife'—a pivotal poem—in which the downpour brings a boyhood recollection floating to the surface: an incident involving his grandfather's knife being retrieved from a river, 'saved from time' as the poem itself preserves the memory. 'I get up... / and write these perishing words down / in the voice of summer rain' another poem ends, while the sprightly 'Envoi' watches his book soar, like a peregrine, 'into the rainy future'. No wonder his poetry acclimatised so readily to its Irish transplantation. With a pen dipped 'in ink mixed with rainwater', Richard Tillinghast has made an indelible mark on both sides of the pond.

from *Sleep Watch* (1969)

The Creation of the Animals

We were angels before the sky lost us
When it happened I touched myself
My hands were new   were not hands
We spoke sounds that no one understood
that were no longer words

He would come and watch our mouths learning the food
he gave us   in love with his own brilliance
Using his power had left him innocent
He thought he had made us from nothing
and we had fallen from the sky like tiles from a mosaic

Later on   when he saw that things had gone wrong
beyond his power to restore them
it rested him to look at us
And I found I could love him in his weakness
as I never could before

I ran on the grass   made paths through the woods
felt the rain in my fur
Remembering the golden cities no longer moves me
I begin to forget   I flew once   and knew the order
of a beauty
I no longer have the mind for.

The Nap

Leaving the alluvial city
when clerks were napping in the fly-blown hockshops
we came by boat to a deep bay
where sunlight gleamed on the brittle water.
A hawk folded and was dying down the wind.
Before his wings changed we dove side by side—
I watch the water break from your arms
sliding away

I feel the breathing
the air shrinking in my body.
Then I breathe out the last of it
and it no longer matters
We are too deep to care

For seven nights
I have come to this city
crossing from the new quarter to the old
by a certain routine they carry out
            without my knowing

It is never as I had remembered—
Smoke pouring from ships in the harbor
                blowing always
        into the old city   stuffing the cries of the water-hawkers.

People are rising to meet it   drinking it into their lungs
as it draws them above the domes and minarets.
The doorways and well-heads are covered with a script I have
        never
I have never seen before   Yet I understand at a glance

the hawk   the crocodile   the fox-headed god.
Never as I had remembered.

I let it go
out of my hands.
You start to move

I kiss your face as it loses the dreams.
Dreams of other nights
                  are something from another life—
      to wake like a mummy in the dead light
words falling from the ceiling
         like snakes through rotten plaster

       Always the same solutions,
something from another life.

The first sounds are the children playing
      hopscotch   jump rope   all their games

R.C.T.

Recruited by my father
I raked romantically
as more leaves fell around me.

They bundled in my arms
            being of one substance with the air,
drifting in the heaped-up gutter.

My father set the pile ablaze
and tended the ragged edges
in a flannel shirt and sleeveless yarn pullover.

His blue-grey
incorruptible eyes
blinked

as the smouldering leaves plunged and
settled in the waver of air.
I watched him growing comfortable

with the blurring remnants
            praising me
and yawning

as the hazy afternoon fell round about him.

Until

I wanted to get you a picture of the room
where the two of them sat always
in the dimness of things: the window seat clouded
by a shorted lamp, the samovar
thick with tea, outdated railway passes
catnip mouse, books piled against the nailed-up door—

Those were some of the things. One of them would strike
days off in bunches, always behind, remarking
"First day of winter", "President Harding
born, 1865". The other one
would sometimes weep over the spectacle, and check
lists arranged for errands repeatedly begun.

Sometimes when water trembled in the drains
and drugs or lack of supper burned the world's dust away,
they saw things their way till the yellow day
and wandered the elated gardens. But mostly
the cat crumpled cellophane
and someone went down for groceries.

No mail came, no offers. Stories below, pedestrians
inched their way antlike through snow that fanned
the vague streetlights with a flutter and stabbing stroke.
No one came stamping through the door, up stairs
and trembling corridors to where
they sat smoking and dazzling the room with talk.

The Keeper

Our animals are sleeping.
The eyes of the dog move   dreaming   his paws
shuffle feebly
about his nose.
And the cat's long sleeping noise
so low as not to be heard, and treble.

I drift in the chair   drowsy
while the others are sleeping,
a family
drawn up in their beds and cosy,
their future devolving on me
as a kindness—the one who answers, the keeper.

Rain on the pavement and roofs of sheds.
One thinks of bluegills slurping gnats
and little frogs among the lily pads.
Time lapses   impossible to picture
the dial of a clock existing anywhere
except perhaps

vastly
the numerals curiously wrought   pale green
against the stars   The hands glide into vision
now here   now there   and scarcely
give the appearance of motion
describing an imaginary plane.

I stare
no farther than my glasses   The mirrored eye
looks through   lidless   having no lash of hair.
Behind the glassy sky
it never closes   or opens,   and keeps
us.   It neither slumbers nor sleeps.

Winter Insomnia

How many winter mornings waking wrongly
at three or four
my mind the only luminosity
in the darkened house . . .

I am alert at once
and think of the cat
coasting on its muscles
from closet shelf to bureau
grave and all-seeing
caring not at all.

Out the windows slowly
a dull light is covering the world's
snow patches and mud ruts,
the neighbour warming up
his car.

Passage

1.

The essence of gasoline is in the streets.
Plastic china is on sale, and cars full of chihuahuas.
In the house with telephones,
no one can see beyond the windows
where taxis cruise,
their headlights mooning on our ceiling
like aquarium lights.

2.

Behind these things   beneath the voices at a fire
is an engine cutting down   all vibration,
the pistons lapsing in their cylinders.
Inside all radiators—the dripping and knocking—
ignoring the stone dome of resonance
where leaded metal sloshes deeply,
must be such a passage as this:
green, inarticulate, subterranean—
seals ducking in and out the waters,
bright-eyed fish breathing upward.

Quieter than the paths of a formal garden,
quieter than a map of New Hampshire,
is this falling off.
We wonder about nothing that does not smooth our eyes.
Here is a single tulip alone, and red.

Impenetrable darkness—
when you pass your hand before your eyes,
there is not even the illusion of sight.
The extinguished lamps are left behind—
one moves by touch
through the narrow sandstone tunnels.
When our cat was gone,
I heard her drowned voice everywhere
crying down the gently sloshing paths of stone.

3.

At night,
in the ocean night
when ever so briefly
we break the water—
down paths of bluish fire
            through clouds of invisible seaweed,
the terrible phosphorous rises for the moon.

Green water   blue water
the bubbles surfacing like marble.
Patterns like smoke rising in a cobalt sky.
Yet they are flat, and sway gently for miles around the ship—
a brightness coming off the air.

Here is a happiness we never know—
the happiness of ants on white paper,
the mind pliant
like blank film lying in solution.

Less Than Yesterday, More Than Tomorrow

Rising from sickness
my bones thin, bending, tender to the touch,
a lightness in the inner ear,

things seem to rush at me.
I huddle away from them, my mother driving—
the street is shocking to the wheels.

They are solicitous, the potted plants
lean towards me, older.
I can see what they were thinking,

They thought . . .
The smiling nurses smiled and looked in all directions
when I was shaved, a necktie, erect on my feet.

Now for a while I possess this room—
the sofa and the fire are mine, lighting the fire
is totally my province.

The floor floats, at sea.
In the window glass lake water, dry leaves floating.
The globe is out of date.

Less and less I feel I am falling forward.
My mother is less patient,
my father will send me to Florida.

For them I am closing the door to the place
where the dead children are stored,
where the pets have gone to Heaven.

The End of Summer in the North

In country churches sheaves of wheat are brought in.
Flowers are laid in the whitewashed sills of deep windows.
As is decent,
the old and sick are taken driving in the country,
afghans and jerseys over their knees.
They praise the sunlight glowing about them through the glass.

Cottage gardens they have never seen before!
Sunflower stems sag helplessly beneath enormous blossoms,
huge dahlias blur their eyes with unheard-of brilliance,
and even the late asters are not homely.

In their cities
people are glad for small favours.
They crowd the parks and spread out over the grass.
Or in an outdoor café, patient with a slow waiter.

A week of rain will kill it,
yet the kitchen help and shop-girls are laughing
through the big square
going home from work in the rain.

They clack their umbrellas along the fence
of the closed amusement park,
and peer through at the rides and concessions.
The boarded windows of the dance pavilion highlight and gleam
like patent leather in the rain.

They see themselves inside still,
as they were,
faces glowing up from the new lagoon
floating beside the upside-down pagoda
and the painted paper lanterns.

Goodbye

for Bob Grenier

When they would wake me before I wanted to
wake
at eleven, the knife-grinder
insisting I shake hands
with someone called "Rhino"

Kept reaching for my watch
Kept losing my ring
Kept diving for my money.
In my inner ear
the long diesels bore down
on New Jersey.

What I loved
was standing at the edge of the subway dock
with trains cascading into the station—
to float for a step or two in the roar
as it carries me off my feet.

Mr _____ was arrested in the lobby
of the fashionable
soaked with
reading a paperback
Inside the black room
(where he was not a guest)

Now it will surely happen
Nothing further to
Wrap him!   not my
—Knocking the faces off, all
over now.

In the Country You Breathe Right

and sleep
in a single breath
the length of the darkness.

Things are
as you remember them—
a calf drinking milk that sloshes through a sieve
a cat running down a well
ferns growing through a roof.
You can hear a leaf
scrape
down the road forty feet.

Everything is wood smoke
and the smell of planked fish.
The fire logs hiss
into the river.

Our shoes are muddy
from when we fed the horses—
wifely, uxorious
they steamed in the March air
as they turned away toward the forest.
My hands are so cold
I hope you can read this.

(for Lucas Myers)

To R,

quand du Seigneur,
from the forest without chairs,

to the shared nowhere of this room
like a treehouse
warm with you in the eye of the storm,
tree trunks elated in the wind,
snow blurting girlishly off the roofs—

submerged, alone,
in the common water and air,
through the eye-struck pool mirror we gaze,
Narcissa-Narcissus.

Are we the two fish
of my dream, sleeping in motion
side by side, cruising
together, helpless?

Will they bury us together?

"Come Home and Be Happy"

1.

Before I know it is there at all
it is all around me.
It lays its hand
on the water in the public fountains.
The air darkens
and a chill goes round my shoulders
like a shawl.

What form will it take for itself
Water running   horses swimming
a flight of birds   a bell   a tower
something that moves in three parts
and turns round on itself?

I sit like this and liken it to a spirit
striking and striking at the whirling void
for entrance.
I start to move
like particles in the field of a magnet.
The buildings radiate,
the broken glass is singing in the street.

"Come back to me and be happy"
it is saying.
It takes me by the arm across years of the closing day
as I run along a grassy ridge   pretending that I am a pony.
It is the time when the long lanes of cars
are switching on their lights—
the rows of white in one direction, and the rows of red.

It is leading me through a storm of oblivion
making my eyes bright with the knowledge
of rooms that no longer exist—
where the yellow shawl before the gas-fire
is keeping the bed from bursting into flame.
The old woman with her whooping laugh
is forcing scrapbooks into my hands.
"You are a true"... etc.

2.

You find yourself
walking
without intention
playing a certain set of streets as a standard opening
or closing . . .

You are drawn past
rows of little shop fronts closing
library assistants making arrangements for supper
parlours being lighted   arms reaching up to close the curtains

The two of you are standing in a rainy field.
Someone watching says aloud
"This is the most beautiful thing I have ever seen"
(the old Budweiser horses?).
She bows her head slightly, steaming in the rain
and starts to walk across the field,
the great hooves graceful as snowshoes in the slush.

You are proud of her beautiful fetlocks
trailing their silky hair in the wet,
as she dreamwalks in the marsh.

"I wear her like a legend round my neck"
you think.
"I will be a cowboy unicorn and squirm at her feet."

At last you enter.
Knowing your shape the walls contract around you.
This is home, she is here.
Wherever you step you inflict a comfortable pain.
Love is real—and you have done the work yourselves,
haven't you—
papered the place in fur.

"Everything Is Going To Be All Right"

This in no way involves calling
the cat you call "Lady"
(and having her come). Nor
cruising the leafy side streets filled with girls,
checking out every one for the one
face . . .

Years ago, lonely for fun
you would stroll and peer into those intelligent interiors
thirsting to penetrate that domesticity—
the white walls, the art books to the ceiling,
the candle for lovemaking . . .
Now that is what you have lived.

The bus that takes you
where you want to go,
where does it take you?
Home to the joys of home,
the daily surrender to being loved.

While you were working, the blizzards moved in and kept
    streaming past the windows
while slowly you made your living by talking.

No one's around—
you leave and
as though the city were a map tilted on its
side you follow all directions
the way a marble does.

To swim in air as snowflakes,
as fish swim in water!—
rising into the midst of brightness
into the snow falling since morning

Snow-mole, headfirst
in the easy, first drifting
feeling the slope coming up to meet you
teasing to spin out
Fine snow ticking into your eyes
out of control
into the drift
iciness
eating your pulse
then just falling, soft
falling   through the clouds.

Did she mean to start you in this
something you lost how long ago?   shadowing
through the deep-tunnelled streets
where you first lived—

Is everything sliding?
Nothing
to worry about—

Getting lost means sliding in all directions.

A Letter

*(about Piero della Francesca's portraits
of the Duke and Duchess of Urbino)*

Was Piero's Duchess of Urbino spoiled
when Berenson used her
for his cover?

He didn't. That's by what's his name   Pollaiuolo.
The impression, though, surfaces continually
as the blue of their sky
becomes in depth the blue of my wall
where they confront each other daily
when the room starts with light
(almost hear a radio).

What did they lack that you and I lacked?
His pose
turning the one unravaged cheek to the artist—
suggests a dignity
we easily find too easy.

Even the well-made bed
of Berenson's description—
"The artist, depicting man disdainful of the storm and stress
of life, is no less reconciling and healing than the poet who,
while endowing Nature with Humanity, rejoices in its measureless
superiority to human passions and human sorrows."
                    —a different world.

There's a simpler way to say this
one feels,
as I lie in the dark—
"If she could do that then,
                    then
(biting the hand she forced to feed her)"—
my limbs neck pillow
like motionless Aztec sculpture
weigh down in their stone solidity . . .

Our life, all the grace of a record-changer . . .
But was there a time—
so different from these nights—
we moved together as we wished
like remembering music?
All I wanted
was music that could care for me.

The landscape background, is it something they wish?
Through hills that float like clouds
in the cloudless sky,
the low walls keep out no one.
The breeze that moves the small boats
over bottomless clear pools
wishes to suspend us forever.
In the washed air attending their impossible heads
nothing could hold us back
from floating in the world of their grace—
radiant as the three pearls of her tiara,
empty as the clear Murano beads she wears.

from *The Knife & Other Poems* (1980)

Return

1.

Sunburst cabbage in grey light
                     summer squash bright as lemons
red tomatoes splitting their skins
            five kinds of chilies burning in cool darkness,
            sunflower lion's-heads
                     in the blue Chevy pickup.

Hands shaking from the cold
            turn on the headlights; he starts
                   down the drive—

A dust you can't see
               settles over the garden and empty cabin

                  silent, unnoticed
                like snow after midnight—

Power shut off in the pump house
            tools suspended over light-blue silhouettes
            he has painted for each of them.

Dark trees stand
            and watch his old truck
                  bump down the hill.

He feels the pecans, the wild hazelnuts
            the small but hard and juicy apples
         in the oversized pockets of his coat,
              the cloth worn soft as rabbit-fur.

White dairy-fences border his way,
                    AM radio farm news,
             placidness of black-nosed sheep in ground fog,
                mist rising over bluegrass.

He drives by Tomales Bay.
             The old fisherman scowls at the low sky and waves,
                   squinting to keep out the
                wreathing, first-cigarette smoke.

             Squirrels
                flash down tree-trunks
when they see him coming—
                          Farmers turn on their lights.

Seeds sprout in the upholstery.
                          Tendrils and runners leap out
                from under his dashboard—

He sails past the whitewashed stumps
                          from the 1906 earthquake,
past the old hotel at Olema,
                   stops for a whizz at Tocaloma,
             because of the name.

                    Sycamore leaves are falling,
                          I feel them rustling
around his shoulders
                and wreathing his hair.

The shepherd with eyes like his
                wakes up in a field.
             The farmer goes out to milk,
             his cold hands pink on the pink freckled udders.

30

The fisherman he could almost be
                    lets down nets into dark water

          and brings up the trout-coloured dawn.

2.

For a few miles on the freeway we
                    float in the same skin,
          he and I.
                    But the sun rises in my
rearview mirror.
          I'm myself now.
I cross the bridge and pay my toll.

The city draws me like a magnet—
                    first the oil refineries,
the mudflats and racetrack by the Bay,
                    the one-story houses,

then a vision of you waking up:
                    cheeks reddening, your black hair long,
your eyes that remind me of Russia,
                              where I've never been—

          as you look out at
                    silvery rain on the fuchsias.

I find your house by feel.
          How many years are gone?
          Your name is gone from the mailbox.
The tropical birds and palm trees and Hawaiian sunset
          you painted with a small brush
are peeling off the beveled glass door.

Forever must be over.
I get into the truck with the good things
        somebody has left here,
                and drive off into the rain—
my left hand asking my right
          "Whose are we?"

The Thief

The thief came down
   through the avenue of dreams.
He took my battered gold,
   my blood-hued jewels from before
      the Revolution—
things I could never get back.

And the vine-covered jungle temple
   that the blind lady told me about:
my sword in one hand,
   in one hand the steaming, bloody virgin heart
         still beating . . .

In the days after,
   on the dusty back roads and crossroads
      in the palms of my hands,
the salt-sweat stars glistened
      at midday;
I felt the speckled wisdom
of East Anglian saints and elders,
   the Word in the shadow of a doorway,
the world swaying in a pail of well-water.

The bees sang in the pines,
     loud in the sunlit open places.

I wake in a cold halo of sweat.
But wasn't I awake already?—
trembling and glancing around in fright
  like deer in the canyon
which also are gone,
crashing off gazelle-like into the trees.

Glass shattered out all around me,
   glass stuck to my fingers,
I'm wiping my eyes—

It's really gone!
I'm sitting up in bed.

Through the huge smashed pane,
         moon over ocean pasture,
Pacific roaring over me.

I'm grinning and bowing like Old Fezziwig
and shaking the hands of flies and bees
   as they pick through the remnants.

Many things that were mine
               are gone.
In my sleep the cat comes purring.
His happiness is, he says,
               as important as mine.
And in sleep comes the thief

leaving me in the care of
the little blind lady in the sunset
and the Chinese postmaster
and the man who says
   "Stay afterward.
I have an introduction for you
that will make everything clear."

Eight Lines by Jalal-ud-din Rumi

Leaving here, I slip out the gates of the palace garden
　　as autumn stuns the trees with remembrance
　　　　　　and makes them come round again

　　　　　　　　　　—a memory of dervish flutes—

In my mind I hear the word *perfect.*
　　　　My feet touch down into cool dust
　　　　　　and my eyes look up
　　to the mountains that ring the high plateau—

Perfect the way air is,
　　including everything there is
　　　　that one can pass through:

　　　The shadow-wings of seabirds
glide over storm-clouds　　forming and dissolving
　　　　　　　　　　turning to the unseen.

And no one really knows
　　what keeps one from going too:

　　　　sleeping under leaves
dissatisfied and hungry　　praying to the Great Light
　　　by day, and to the Moon, Our Lady—

　　　My only friends were the wolves.

A shadow fell from the old-fashioned porch light,
　　called my name into the trees,
and promised to buy me everything.

I was held by the thought of return
   and went back far enough to hear the music,
            that was once so much a part—
      but the cold wind
            blew it out of my heart.

I crept unseen one rainy night
         into their carriage,
and caressed them in the likeness of warmth
   while they talked happily and drove.

Yet the wind today
         spreads yellow leaves across the road
   so familiar in the way it disappears
      over hills the colour of sky—

And the whirlwind dervish voices blow
      over desolate stone:

Come, come again, whoever you are
   —wanderer, worshipper, lover of leaving—
            it doesn't matter.
      Ours is not a caravan of despair.
Come even though you have broken your vows
                        back there

      a thousand times—
            Come once more.

The Knife

for David Tillinghast

What was it I wonder?
   in my favourite weather   in the driving rain
      that drew me like a living hand
What was it
   like a living hand
that spun me off the freeway
   and stopped me
on a side street in California
with the rain pelting slick leaves down my windshield

to see the words of my brother's poem
   afloat on the bright air,
   and the knife I almost lost
      falling end over end through twenty years
               to the depths of Spring River—

the knife I had used to cut a fish open,
               caught in time
   the instant where it falls
            through a green flame of living water.

My one brother,
            who saw more in the river than water
who understood what the fathers knew,
               dove from the Old Town canoe
   plunged and found his place
               in the unstoppable live water

seeing with opened eyes
          the green glow on the rocks
                    and the willows running underwater—
          like leaves over clear glass in the rain—

While the long-jawed, predatory fish
   the alligator gar
watched out of prehistory
   schooled in the water like shadows
          unmoved in the current,
watched unwondering.

          The cold raw-boned, white-skinned boy
     curls off his dive in deep water
          and sees on the slab-rock
filling more space than the space it fills:

          the lost thing   *the knife*
     current swift all around it

and fish blood denser than our blood
   still stuck to the pike-jaw knife blade
which carries a shape like the strife of brothers
                    —old as blood—
     the staghorn handle smooth as time.

          Now I call to him
               and now I see
     David burst into the upper air
gasping as he brings to the surface our grandfather's knife
          shaped now, for as long as these words last,
               like all things saved from time.

I see in its steel
  the worn gold on my father's hand
            the light in those trees
  the look on my son's face   a moment old

      like the river   old like rain
  older than anything that dies can be.

Hearing of the End of the War

for Joshua Tillinghast

1.

Clouds dissolve into blueness.
              The Rockies float like clouds
        in the shimmery blue heat.

The moon floats there still
              like some round marble relic,
its classic face rubbed away by time.

A stranger arrives, all the way from Denver.
              We feed him.
He tells us that the war is over.

For years I have stopped to wonder
              what it would feel like now.
And now I only hear the slight noise
              the moment makes,
        like ice cracking,
as it flows behind me into the past.

2.

I go to the well
              and draw up a bottle of my homemade beer.
The coldness from thirty feet down
              beads out wet on the brown bottle.

Breathing dusty pine fragrance,
            I pop open the beer, and drink
till my skull aches from the coldness.

Rubbed white dust is on plum skins
                as they ripen.
                        Green wild blueberries
                grow from the rocks.

Wind blows in off the peaks,
                    high in the dust-flecked sun-shafts
            that light up the dark trees.
Rustlings and murmured syllables from other days
                pass through and linger
                and leave their ponies
    to roam among the trees and graze the coarse grass
                off the forest floor.

Treetop breezes, and voices
                returning home
from a fight somebody lost in these mountains
                a hundred and ten years ago—

A horse cries out,
                loose in the woods,
                        running and free.
His unshod hooves thud
                on the hard-packed dirt.

And then each sound drops away
    —like a dream you can't even remember—

deep behind the leaves of the forest.

3.

From bark-covered rafters
　　white sheets hang squarely down,
dividing the still afternoon into rooms
　　　　where we sleep, or read,
　　　or play a slow game of hearts.

Everyone is unbuttoned and at their ease.

　　　The baby's clear syllables
　　　　　rise into space:
　　milky　　like the half-moons
　　on his tiny fingernails,

　　　　　finer than fine paper.

A new life breathes in the world—
　　　　fragile, radiant,
　　　unused to the ways of men.

From halfway down the valley
　　　bamboo flute noises rise　　float
　　　　　flutter
　　　　　and shatter
　　against the Great Divide.

Aspens and a Photograph

Winding down from fourteen thousand feet
through melting slush and Rocky Mountain tundra,

white flesh of new aspens—
                    and a photograph I still see
            from an attic in Trinidad,
                    Colorado.

Around bends in the road,
                    between the blue distances of sky,
            coveys of aspen.
Their leaves flutter all at once in the wind:
                    small wing-beats in fear.

Green aspens—tall, root-tough,
  wind-graced and swayed in the blustery weather.
Right up against granite,
            saplings springing up through snow.

The photograph:
two girls' faces from 1881
in a house that raised six generations on silver—
their black gowns, aprons, their Chinese embroidery—
            only daughters
                    smiling thinly into the black camera,
holding in their laps, as a kind of joke,
            long-barreled pistols.

Shooting Ducks in South Louisiana

for David Tillinghast and in memory of R.C. Tillinghast

The cold moon led us coldly
  —three men in a motorboat—
down foggy canals before dawn
        past cut sugarcane in December.

        Mud banks came alive by flashlight.
Black cottonmouth moccasins
  —the length of a man in the bayou—
slid into black water, head high,
  cocky as you might feel
stepping out on Canal Street
  going for coffee at 4 A.M.
          at the Café du Monde.

An Indian trapper called to us
  from his motorised pirogue,
        Cajun French on his radio—
taking muskrat, swamp rat, weasel,
      "anything with fur".

Marsh life waking in the dark:
gurgling, sneaking, murdering, whooping—
  a muskrat breast-stroking through weeds toward food,
      his sleek coat parted smooth by black satin water—
frogs bellowing, bulbous water lilies adrift
      cypresses digging their roots into water-borne ooze
dark juices collapsing cell-walls,
      oil rigs flaring thinly at daybreak.

Light dawned in our hunting-nerves.
We called to the ducks in their language.
They circled, set wing, glided into range.
        Our eyes saw keener.
Our blood leaped. We stood up and fired—
        and we didn't miss many that day,
                piling the boat between us with mallards.

The whole town of Cutoff ate ducks that Sunday.
        I sat in the boat,
                bloody swamp-juice sloshing my boots,
                        ears dulled by the sound of my gun,—
and looked at a drake I had killed:
        sleek neck hanging limp,
                        green head bloodied,
                raucous energy stopped.
I plucked a purple feather from his dead wing,
and wore the life of that bird in my hat.

Lost Cove & The Rose of San Antone

Evening comes on. I put on a clean white shirt
and feel how well it fits me. I pour bourbon,
with spring water from a plastic jug,
and look out sliding glass doors
at green suburban hills blurred with smog.
Two watches lie on the table before me:
one set for now, one telling time in 1938,
their glass faces reflecting the round California sky.

The man I see through the eye of the second watch
sits in a silence too deep for my nerves
and stares out at twilight
fading on trunks of pine and oak.
The black Model-A car rusts into the stream
that runs past his cabin in Lost Cove, Tennessee.
He reaches for the whiskey on the table,
and his sleeve clears a path through pine-needles and dust.

The coal that tumbles out of his hillside
soils the air and brick houses in Nashville.
Words burn in the rain there
from the power of water that runs past his door.
He looks at his watch and turns on the radio.
The music reaches him, all the way from Nashville.
He holds his glass of whiskey up to the light
that is almost gone. Its colour suits his thoughts.

The fiddles and autoharp fill up the dark room
and push out through paint-blackened screens
into black oaks that press against the house.
His face hurts me. It doesn't look right.
He goes against the grain
of whiskey he has made himself, and rides
the wire-song of a steel guitar through small towns,
through the bug-crowded air of farm-crossings late at night.

The disembodied, high guitar line swims in his nerves
like a salmon up a flint-rock stream,
falls like a hawk on blood.
The whiskey burns and soothes.
His tongue starts to move to the words of the song:
trains and big woods and bottomless rivers,
hard drinking, broken hearts, and death.
His blood knows whose song this is.

He's never swum in no bottomless river,
or rode that night train to Memphis,
or sat and stared at those thirteen unlucky bars.
But he sees the moon rise, with the Rose of San Antone
tattooed on it in blood.
A waitress in Denver glides toward him with drinks on a tray.
He stumbles, drunk, through strange woods by an airport
and walks out in San Francisco with a gun in his pocket. . . .

The moon sets, over hills cold and unfamiliar.
I shut off the radio, and hear the sea-roar of the freeway.
Who is this man I have dreamed up?
I cork the bottle, and get up and lock the door.

Things Past

for Maurya and Tamara Simon

Ten years into memory, a house
  in the bright fluid
time—dark grain of walnut, dark
women's bodies
        in paintings by sisters.

1632 Walnut Street:
  the solid multiples of eight
  like a vintage Oldsmobile,
the curves of the numbers,
  the porch, the porch-roof lighted,
shaped a little by memory—
  lit up like a jukebox,
like an old-fashioned sunset.

Wood-doves murmur in the eaves
        as we wake.
Leaf-shadows   sun-circles
  glide over the white ceiling
    from outside our lives.

On the white terrace
  Ruthie brushes out her thick hair
        straight and blond.
Between storms: January sunlight
  rare cloud-rainbows
    the air like a telescope
trained on the rain-wet Berkeley hills.

Mexican smoke curls
over the drifting walnut grain.
Sisters, Maurya and Tamara
    sketch, sing, cook.

I drive by the house in the rain
        tonight
and see myself at the kitchen table.
As I write,
   my notebook rests on an open cookbook.
My beard curls
        in the steamy air
of Christmas turkey soup they are cooking.

Janis Joplin still sings   *Love*
                is like a ball and chain!
The guitar solo
            cuts through the years
like a pulsating river of acid.

They're drinking coffee together,
        and talking about the weather
  that squally, blowsy Berkeley night.
I can hardly see myself
   for the steam gathering on the glass.

Borders, Woven Goods, and the Rhythm Behind All Things

for Paul Portugés and Maureen Riley

The barbs on the barbed-wire fence
that bordered my land in misty rain
burned evilly
      through second-growth redwoods.
Deer season: rifle fire in the woods.
The border wind was thick, and colder than reality,
smelling of murder, of the Percys and Douglasses
and the troubles in the North.

Maureen made me take off the cap
she had knitted me.
"It's too bright," she said.

The world came apart for the second time.
Benjy stampeded the cattle toward us
with border-dog instincts
curled tight in his fur
like the smoke of fugitive campfires
clinging in highland wool.
Benjy's gold coat shimmered
like a gold Kathmandu temple-dog as he ran.
With new-found double vision I saw the cattle charge—
their spirits next to them
like their shadows—,
bright outlines of blizzard.
We sheltered in that circular
scrub-redwood grove
halfway up the ridge

in the huge, upland, rock-filled pasture,
watching from trees
as they ghosted past with thunder.

"Woven goods are the secret,"
I told you and Maureen gravely.
We were "like family".
"We can't help you,"
you both said sensibly,
and let me lose my mind alone.

Real estate schemes
were the life-force of America,
from Washington on—
the California landscape told me
as I drove up Thursday after work.
The brakes on my little foreign car
slipped on Thursday's cheap, flimsy hills
and steep grades up and down
the road to Point Reyes.

On the radio Bob Dylan was moaning:
When you're lost in the rain in Juarez
and it's Eastertime too!
And your gravity fails
and negativity won't pull you through!

Feather-foot, wing-guided
to her little house down the road,
emerging wide-open from the creek,
the Sonoma remnant of the once-vast forest of redwoods
that grew from San Francisco north to Canada—
to be welcomed as a ghost always expects to be,
with salads from the garden,
love, no questions, old wine.

No, I went on that trip alone.
I rolled in the mud and cow-dung.
I threw away *The Purpose of Life,*
by Hazrat Inayat Khan,
and never found it again.
I lay there in the mire all afternoon
wondering who I was,
watching weekend traffic below on the highway.

My eyesight got perfect
my glasses lost or broken.
I could see everything, 360°,
but I couldn't see who it was
who was seeing it.
Borders, knit, woven things,
the Sunday drivers down below me.
The rhythm of motors.

I clicked my teeth together
and found a rhythm—
one, then two, then two and two—
and that brought me back into the world.

Woven things. They are warmer than skins.
I like to think of the person who unravelled that,
twisting together sheep's wool and thistles
on some hillside in the early pastoral age.

I walk out in thought with you tonight, Paul,
in the hills where I know you wander,
in the chaparral over Santa Barbara,—
and with you, Maureen,
working at your flower stand, paying for your house . . .
Maybe you see me for a moment in the eyes of a customer.
I see Benjy's proud jaws

on buses in Mexico, "the protector",
when you were pregnant with Amin,—
his silk, curly coat
and his border ancestry.

This is what I wanted to say:
The family is what there is.
Woven things are warmer than skins.
All life is rhythm.
At borders, think.

I think the cows ate that knitted cap.

Sovereigns

after Rilke

The sovereigns of the world are old,
and die without heirs.
Their pale sons die behind guarded doors.
Their daughters yield weak crowns to violence;
they break in the rough hands of the people.
The haughty, beef-cattle faces bleed
  into eagles and hammers.

New money, new metal, new rulers—
the old glitter just beyond reach:
rows of decorations on white dress uniforms.
They reincarnate as gears
to turn the machine of the world.

But luck is beyond possessing.

The metal is wild, and homesick.
Each day is one day less
until it disappears
from the mints and factories
that show it so poor a life.
From bank-vaults, from inside clocks,
in dreams it runs again
through slow arteries inside mountains.
The heart pauses,
and pumps it back to the source.

Summer Rain

Summer rain, and the voices of children
        from another room.
Old friends from summers past,
we drink old whiskey and talk about ghosts.
The rain ebbs, rattles the summer cottage roof,
  soaks the perished leaves in wooden gutters,
then gusts and
        drowns our fond talk.
It's really coming down, we chatter,
  as though rain sometimes rose.

The power fails.
We sit in darkness, under the heavy storm.
Our children—frightened, laughing—
  run in to be beside us.

The weak lights surge on.
We see each other's children newly.
How they've grown!   we prose
with conventional smiles, acceptingly commonplace,
  as they go back to playing.
Yet growing is what a child does.

And ourselves?
You haven't changed a bit,
  we not exactly lie,
meaning the shock is not so great
        as we'd expected.
It's the tired look around the eyes,
the flesh a little loose on the jaw . . .

Your oldest daughter's a senior at Yale.
We're like our grandparents and our parents now,
        shocked by the present.
We say goodnight. I can hardly lift
        my young son anymore
as I carry him to the car asleep.

The rain comes down, comes down, comes down.
One would think it would wear the earth away.
You told us about a skeleton
        you awoke seeing—
the dawn light on the bone.
It wakes me this morning early.
But I'm sure it wasn't a ghost, you said
        in your sensible way,
It was just my terrible fear of death.

Rain roars on the broad oak leaves
  and wears away the limestone.
I smell the mildewed bindings
  of books I bought as a student.
How shabby, how pathetic they look now
  as they stand there on their shelves unread!
Children are all that matters, you said
  last night, and I agreed.
The children's play-song—repetitive, inane—
  keeps sounding in my head.
I get up—last night's spirits alive
  this morning in my blood—
and write these perishing words down
in the voice of summer rain.

Views of the Indies

for Charles

> *In the kingdom of Jah*
> *Man shall reign.*

1.

Azure tropical sky
reflections   in an ocean as green
     as a swimming pool.

Clouds of mist in green camphor trees,
     tin roofs sloping up to mountains.
Miles of refuse and a city.

A cow munching newspapers
     wobbles in traffic—
a hollow carcass blown up with air,
     brushing with her ribs
Chevrolets and Plymouths from the 50s,
     red noise   radio speakers on poles playing bhajan
mangoes stacked in ripe dust.

Pigs root up filth
     out of cracks in the pavement;
a little girl shepherds them.

Blessed are the poor,
     somebody says,
for they live on fire and air—
     weed-cigarettes   cheap rum
       crime   TV
and the white moon,
     its edges sharp as broken glass.

A squadron of B-52s
        plays a Bach cantata
in a church made entirely of bones.

Blessed are the weak,
for they have to get strong in a hurry.

2.

        Dust-skinned men
    Peacock feathers   matted hair
spirit-legs chalk-brown
        gums betel-nut red
    bad looking eyes.
        They carry a litter.
They hurry   over hard-packed dirt
past tough-rooted old ghosts of trees
        down winding streets.
    The body they carry—
insubstantial bundle of orange cloth
        roped to saplings.
The wind turns around:
    hair burning   burning flesh.

Vultures float
        on the heavy air.

Fires to dispose of the dead.

Boats full to the river with firewood,
    the far bank of the river vague in brown haze.
        Long barges glide past
    with quarried marble and tin ore
        for the mother country.

Attendants circle the blazes,
      men the missionaries never met—
long poles in their hands to crack bones,
      harsh, glittering cymbals,
faces chapped by fire,
        yellow hundreds of candles
    eyes shiny, black, unfocussed.
They stoke up their *ganja* pipes with live coals
      off the funeral pyres.

    Gongs beat the thick air.
Black goddess enthroned on a dead steer.
Black skulls explode in bloodshot eyes.

Souls die in those fires—
        or do the greasy smoke and incense
  the funeral coins clutched in dead hands,
    weird chants of holy widows from riverbank temples,
carry them clear over the wide, bending river?

3.

Like Monarch butterflies the souls glide
      through a garden
where the animals worship them
    and call them the first woman and man.
Now the voice of God.
Now sweat pours down to water the cane.

High lightning zig-zags across the darkness.
The storm breaks   monkeys scream
   and crash off into the bush.

The jungle parts around brown, smooth faces:
Indians
seeing for the first time
the City—
their liquid eyes suddenly still.

Rain beats down brown smoke
from cooking fires on mud,
darkens the stone colonial prison
heavy in the mist—
skyscraper walls of corporate glass,
white crosses of missionary churches
over rain-slick banana leaves,—
like a tragic warning
from the incomprehensible past.

Power surges on and off
through low-voltage bulbs in palm trees,
throwing dark rainbows into the steamy night.
The Indians look into each other's eyes
and laugh their musical laugh,
and push each other in play.
They ask, in their birdlike tongue,
the way to the marketplace.

from *Sewanee in Ruins* (1981)

Sewanee in Ruins, Part I

The Romantics were right.
Gothic buildings are best seen in ruins:
sky-sprung clerestories in wild brambles,
Romanesque arches reconstructed by the mind,
tumbled-over stones to stumble on in a field
of grey violets,
in a place you can no longer drive to.

When I walk by the neo-Gothic
duPont Library at the University of the South,
its new stone rouged-up, peachy
after October rain,
my mind sees the facade stripped of half its masonry
by Virginia creeper and torn fog.
I smile into leaves of the bramble stock,
strong and ugly,
aggressively shiny in the mist.

But I come from the cemetery,
where the past is buried under stone.
I smile into the broad, pleasant faces of my students,
the black among the white
—for we are one people—;
yet my thoughts are with men I have heard of and read of
who, possessed by a fatal romanticism,
killed at fourteen,
ate corn burned in the field,
and wore the dead enemies' shoes
in 1865, when everything burned
but the brick chimneys
and a way of talking.

I touch with my tongue my four gold teeth,
answer to the name *Sir*,
and feel out of place
in my twenty-year-old tweeds
among these boys and girls
who call themselves men and women,
these ripe-peach bodies and untouched smiles,
these peacock-blue, canary-yellow, billiard-table-green
clothes from the catalogue of L.L. Bean—
initials emblazoned as on silver—
and hundreds of tiny alligators that never snap.

I climb the 1890s Gothic battlements to my classroom
and teach these fortunate young men and women
their history,
and the old lost nation's name for this spot:
Rattlesnake Springs.
Two coiled rattlesnakes spelled into a slab of rock.

Saawaneew in Algonquin,
though white men didn't know it,
meant The South,
from the Ohio to the Gulf of Mexico.

The words of someone's old diary or letter from 1860:
Nine bishops in their robes
and 50 or 60 clergymen in surplices and gowns
and some 5,000 people
formed a procession
and headed by a band playing Hail Columbia
marched to the spot
where the main building of the university
was to be.
Here Old Hundred *was sung by the vast multitude.*

Those confident, cotton-flush Southerners,
fifty years from the wilderness,
with their horse races, cockfights, African slaves,
their code of duello and decanter,
their railroad cars full of Sir Walter Scott romances,
their 19th-century optimism
and half a million cotton dollars as endowment,
founded *their "Southern Oxford",*
as they always called it.

The hogsheads of hams, the barrels, and boxes, and bags
of groceries, the cartloads of crockery and glass, the
bales of sheeting and blankets, and acres of straw beds,
indicated that Southern hospitality for once
had entered upon the difficult undertaking
of outdoing itself. . . .

Yet even then,
there was a feeling as of a great danger
near at hand,
a yawning chasm which all feared to look upon. . . .

Next April
the bells of St Philip's and St Michael's,
the old Charleston churches,
change-rang in celebration.
But a clearheaded observer, if one could be found,
looking off the Battery past Fort Sumter
into the immense ocean and sky,
must have felt mostly dread.

The rest of the oft-told tale is too well known,
how war devastated the land
the two armies passed over, fighting as they went.

The frame houses
built for Bishops Elliott and Polk
have been burnt to the ground,
the cornerstone blasted to pieces by Federal stragglers—
the six-ton block of marble
that 34 yoke of oxen
had dragged up the mountain from Elk River.

We are encamped (21st Indiana Infantry)
on the top of the Cumberland Mountains,
on the site of the grand Southern University
that was to have been. . . .
Near our quarters is a very large spring
of the clearest and finest water I ever drank.
We expect no real fight between here and Atlanta.

My pleasant-faced freshmen
from South Carolina, Texas, Kentucky, Alabama
laugh at the word *Yankee,*
considering my use of it a kind of local colour.
To them the Great War of the Sixties
is like some football game we lost.

And I have no quarrel with them.

To wear expensive clothes,
to enjoy wearing them
—or just not to think about it—,
to go through the seasons as from one party to the next,
to know no enemies,
to turn from boy or girl May- or June-like
into man or woman,
to make 18-year-old love in the back seat of a Cadillac
on a warm Delta night—
this is the way to be young!

Not to ride and kill with Forrest all across Tennessee
or die with Jackson at Chancellorsville
or Polk at Piney Mount,
or come back from war
with health and nerves and worldly goods destroyed.
The privilege of being young,
the luxury of ignoring history—
this is what their great-great-grandfathers fought for,
though they lost.

For the flaw in their neo-classical structure—
the evil of owning human beings—,
they paid, all of them and all of us,
punished by a vengeance only New England could devise—
though only three Tennesseans out of a hundred in 1860
had owned a slave.

The Armies of Emancipation,
having *loosed the fateful lightning*
of His terrible swift sword,
would be free to go West and kill Indians.
The machines tooled in that war economy
eased the North on plush velvet and iron rails
into its Gilded Age,
and reconstructed the South
with sharecropping and hunger—
and a deeper thirst,
not satisfied by the Coke you drink
flying Delta over kudzu fields out of Atlanta,
reading *The Last Gentleman* by Walker Percy.

History stopped in 1865,
then started again as memory:
the grey and gold of the good-smelling broadcloth uniform,
the new, beautiful, hand-sewn battle flag,
the West Point strategists, the Ciceronian orations,
the cavalry charges—
soldiers on a road sing "Away, Away"—;
then the heads shot off friends' shoulders,
the desertions, the belly-killing stench of dead flesh,
the forced marches over hardscrabble Virginia roads—
and Richmond like a brick graveyard.

from *Our Flag Was Still There* (1984)

Our Flag Was Still There

for Hamza

For music, "Victory at Sea", or "In the Mood".

"Chessie", the Chesapeake and Ohio's
advertising mascot, snoozes
under sixty-mile-per-hour lamplight.
Two tabby kittens gaze saucer-eyed at their tomcat dad,
who sits alertly on his haunches,
soft field cap cocked to one side above neat,
pleasure-pursed lips and regimental whiskers.
One paw bandaged.
A Congressional Medal of Honour
red-white-and-blue-ribboned around his neck.
As convincingly at attention as a military-style,
family-oriented cat can be in a pullman car.
On his well-groomed chest, rows of campaign ribbons.
A dignified, "can do" look
hovers about his muscled smile.

In the luggage rack, a U.S. combat helmet
and a rising-sun flag in tatters.

I had a flag like that.
One of my three red-headed Marine cousins
brought it back from the South Pacific.
I thumbtacked it to the wall of my room.
The Japanese who had fought under it
perished in fierce firestorms.
They and their flag went up in that conflagration.

Our flag was still there.
Against a backdrop of blue sky and innocent clouds,
a line of six blunt-nosed P-47 fighters—
boxy and powerful like the grey Olds
we bought after the War
and drove to the Berkshires for the summer—
flew off on a mission to Corregidor.
The flag, unfurled in the stiff breeze,
was superimposed over the line of airplanes
on the cover of the Sunday magazine
one June morning in 1943.
The wind that made it wave as it does in pictures
blew off long ago toward China.

The sun nooned over orange groves and beaches.
Sparks from welding torches
illuminated the sleep of the City of the Angels
and darkened the sleep of others
as women workers beside the men
lowered masks over their faces,
and the children of New Jersey and Mississippi,
Europe and Detroit,
laboured to make aluminum fly
and set afloat fleets of destroyers
and submarines radaring to the kill.

Looking ahead, there was a world of bluegrass lawns,
panelled wood enamelled white, grandparents' faces
rosy over reassuring, hand-rubbed bannisters,
Yale locks, brass door-knockers, hardwood floors,
the odour of good furniture and wax,
a holiday design of holly leaves and berries on a stiff card,
a little girl holding gift packages as big as she is,
a boy, a real boy, bright as a new penny.

But now, in '43, the men and women pulled apart
like the elders of some stern, taboo-ridden tribe,
putting off till after the War the lives
of those who in twenty-five years
stood baffled on the 4th of July among uncles,
drove good German cars,
floated in tubs of hot, redwood-scented water with friends,
and greeted each other with the word, "Peace".

Fossils, Metal, and the Blue Limit

for Charles

"Thou anointest my head with oil."

The sky, out of reach, unexpected,
like the domed ceiling of a mosque—
us motoring up the long freeway
north from San Francisco:
a promise, yes, a blue ribbon.

We navigate privileged space in the fast lane,
two men and two boys in a Volkswagen van,
alongside families getting a jump on the weekend heat
in cushy, portable, air-conditioned interiors
that rolled down suburban drives
hours and miles ago.
My big, hot-rodded, 1700-cubic-centimetre engine revs
fast, loud, and *comme il faut;*
the van lunges eagerly northstate

breezing through a river of air—
inches above the concrete slabs that,
dovetailed by sky-coloured slicks of asphalt, *are*
the freeway.

Three fibreglass poles and a nine-foot, willowy fly rod
of the lightest material made
bounce easily to the even pace of the engine
as my customised classic
1966 VW Microbus, forest green
with white trim,
or as I might call it
in moments of gloom,

"decrepit old wreck",—
burns through the blue fumes
with bumper stickers advising contradictorily "Bomb Iran"
and "Think Trout"
Tolstoy would have loved it.

Everything the round eye sees
suggests the absence of limitation
as we uncork the day with coffee and Bushmill's—
even what the shapeless, mind's eye
imagines and recalls:
the view to limestone in the pine-shadowed creek
under Mount Lassen,
our destination;
even the fat, springy, uncoiling, muscular
earthworms I dug at first light out of odourous humus
with a clean-tined pitchfork.

Ayub, né Borsky,
companion on many an outing,
fair or foul, poaching or sport, trout or shark—:
street artist, carpenter, taxi driver, mystic, bad cook,
with a face like a rained-on rock,—
rolls a cigarette out of thick, dark
Dutch tobacco,
smokes it through his Mosaic beard
(his grey hair thin, stretched and stranded,
three wavy pencil-lines over his crown),
and gives his well-considered philosophy of life
and trout
to his two sons,
Eric—dark, humourous, fourteen,
maker of fine model airplanes—
and Dylan—blond, ten—:

about "feeding stations", about how
the big trout take the choicest spots
("Just like you, Dad"),
how they face upstream, treading icy water,
and don't blink—
about the trout's "window of vision"
wherein the fisherman looms huge, dark, and threatening
("Just like you again, Dad")
unless he treads softly, and relies on concealment—
and how "the freeway is a river",
the cars swimming in four diverted and weaving currents,
how everything is like that really,
and how—

Quick as a rainbow trout
flashes sunlight
out of a deep pool—
right at the top of a grade past Cloverdale,
the green warning signal on the dash flickers
and stays lit!
Blue smoke congregates behind us,
I veer across two lanes,
slide to a stop on the sandy shoulder,
hood
(in the back in a Volkswagen, remember?)
up,
head under hood,
smoke in eyes:
OIL! the engine-opening black
as the underground streams
of Arabia, black
as the fingernails and secret dreams
of the Ayatollah.

We glut it with an extra quart, then another,
and point it toward the exit
though it smokes
like a pointillist painting of London weather
and early Marxist pollution-stacks.
Like those long first paragraphs of *Bleak House*,
creeping, deliberate, ominous,
we nose the cloud
into the town of Weed
along a cyclone fence and frontage road,
up a little paved crescent of street,
then down another one, plain and straight,
in view of the bleached, horizontal, meandering river—
then straight down, miraculously, a yarrow-wild drive:
two wheel-thin slabs of concrete wheelwise
downhill, beside an abandoned, pink, shotgun house.

Down a slanting, weed-jungled drive,
beside a pink house that is having no trouble
falling apart,
under two shapely, identical camphor trees
and one disreputable sycamore,
next to a grey picket fence and a rained-on, broke-down couch,
we squat on our heels like aborigines
sun-squinting at the engine: black, oil-flooded.
Groping behind it blind I scorch
the first, second, third knuckles on overheated steel,
grabbing for the burst, expensive cooler hose
splashing black fossil-oil
over every inch of metal,
where it burns off as blue smoke
into the clogged atmosphere.

My Piscean friend grins
in the dirty face of disaster.
(Of course it is not his car.)

Hi-temp rubber hose, this size (handing it),
and three quarts 30-weight oil—
the boys are out of the van then,
skateboarding down the long street.
"The sky's the limit"
is the thought I imagine
for them.
For us, a problem, a headache, gloom.

We take in the panorama
of blue-collar suburbia:
cheap, 1950s houses
dwarfed more even than they anyway would be
by "recreational vehicles", evil-looking, smoked-glass vans,
reptilian-fendered hot rods, a vintage Airstream
trailer, jacked-up
Camaros and Mustangs, souped-up
otherworldly Harleys with chrome out to here,
a single, monstrous, ark-sized, blunt-nosed speedboat,
ready to lumber off into the next flood.

Then a (unique in my experience) residential used-car lot,
and a thirtyish, drunkish ex-biker
with a jack to rent—
slouched in the doorway
with "Born to Lose" and "WHITE
ON" and prison-art swastikas
tattooed asymmetrically across his belly,
latitude unknown, longitude uncertain,
where "Save the Whales"
would have seemed more appropriate.
"Hitler's Revenge", he calls my car.
I see the look of concern
drift across my face,

mirrored in the blue sky
of his mirror shades.

But everything's cool!

The procedure:
battery disconnected, jittery, wires pulled
off and labeled with bits of brown tape.
Yank off the gas-line, gas spurts,
choke it fumblingly with an old pencil (not knowing
to clamp it first
with your small vise-grip),
and it dangles there sealed—
pass the Bushmill's around
(cuts the fumes):
then to get the bumper and assorted pieces of tin,
cunningly shaped,
from around the engine, then,
passing the big wrench back and forth between us,
and dropping it once, twice, clangingly on cement:
four nuts haltingly and bothersomely
twisted off the engine-studs,
while the neighbours—two Bahai housewives,
the over-the-hill Angel, and an off-duty postman—
drink beer and make free with advice,
we ease, rock, nudge
the engine onto the ton-and-a-half
Hein-Becker floor-jack,
hulking and out of place,
mired and sliding already
in the sweet grass
becoming mud.

The disconnected engine broods there like a primal force,
the metal like a fifth element,
like an alien life-form from a slower planet
putting in downtime,
earth-morning becoming midday
as the metal ticks and bangs, cooling, contracting,
under twin camphor trees and sky.

Were days like this foreseen
in the Platonic heaven of machinists?
or by the generations of men,
with boots and soiled caps and wire-rimmed eyeglasses
and daughters and sons,
who brought iron ore out of the earth,
learned to smelt it, and formed it into steel,
then refined oil to cool
every frictive articulation of that wonder,
an apparatus (1637) *for applying mechanical power,*
consisting of a number of parts, each
having a definite function,—
which they had named Machine?

The day heats up,
mare's-tails braid across the blue.
The boys skate back into sight down the long, straight street
exhilarated, with motor oil and lengths of hose.
Now, pull the old hoses off,
fit the new ones on true,
tighten the clamps to a turn,
pump the jack,
grunt, puff, and stagger,
bring the boys and neighbours into it,
struggle, despair, and struggle
to work the heavy, lumbering mass of old technology

onto the four, eccentrically placed engine-studs,
tighten the four nuts back on,
cross-eyed with concentration,
feeling humbly resigned
and at the same time in some sense weirdly lucky,
that nothing worse than this
has gone wrong,
fit
the tin back on,
hook up the gas line,
plug the wires back in,
replace the bumper, and our job is done.

Now the blond, virgin oil
inside the newly tight engine.
Now I reach out my hand
and turn the key.
The engine kicks to life,
no oil leaks,
the stream awaits.
In a moment, you who read this,
you can drive it to the carwash and clean it up for me.

My hand, arm, shoulder muscles rebound
with freedom, reflexively,
from the work they have done:
and the quaint construance of the word nut
which follows its botanical meanings
in the Oxford English Dictionary
(I wish I had it right here at my elbow)—
a small block of wood, iron, etc.,
pierced, and wormed with a female screw—
drifts into my mind,
suggesting the history, and the slow romance
of machinery.

Maybe what I mean to say is the way oil
looks on skin:
black, verging on chemically murky translucence,
the little human hairs bravely standing up half-bent
beneath the grime, the irreducible petro-dirt—
or maybe it's what is going to happen
to Joe Borsky,
how two weeks from now
he will take a knife in the gut
and be in all the papers
as he and the passenger in his cab
go after a man who is trying to rape a nurse
as she goes home from work
on Nob Hill at four in the morning.

He's one of the lucky ones, however:
only his flesh is wounded.
He'll soon recover.

Waiting for you,
so we can get on up the road,
I loaf here in the bruised, oil-shiny grass,
with a green pen that writes blue,
while my friend meditatively smokes,
as unaware as I am of what lies ahead of him.
The boys are quiet now, the neighbours
have gone home
with their jack, their help, and their noise.
Smells of crushed grass, beer, hot oil, scorched metal
hang in the air.
I hear the river
loop and crook back on itself
over its sandy-bottomed channel
through the nearby field,

where shattered cinderblocks
and an old drive-train sprawl.

Between the river and the sky,
the mountains:
the Sierra—a myth, a truth,
the hard backbone of the West,
distances extending untravelled
a thousand miles or more from here
up switchbacked roads
with pine needles dusted over them,
over daylong, empty deserts,
past granite diners that say more about loneliness
than will easily go into words—
to the eastern slope of the Rockies,
half of America away.

Stained with the bodies of half-billion-year-old plants,
releasing my breath upward,
I stare upward uncomprehendingly
at the blue, cloud-woven limit of the sky.

Easter Week: Vermont

in memory of Robert Fitzgerald

Snowbanks, exhausted, melt onto pavement.
Slick stripes on the road, buttercup yellow—
A pickup truck that colour, and a sign,
Diamond-shaped, "Frost Heaves", stuck in grey snow.

In graveyards, around tombstones, snow scooped, cupped,
Around named, sun-thawed granite and marble.
The trees, from within, push back the snowdrifts.
Maybe in wild trout today the blood moves.

Maples, five feet through, drain into buckets.
A white-haired man, his black-and-red-checked back
To me, lumbers through timber with buckets full.
Steam spouts out the tops of sugar-houses.

New birch saplings by the roadside stare
With a coldness from inside the bark
That goes back a hundred million winters.
Their nerve has survived another freeze.

The bare ground, snow-covered since November,
Turns up filter-tips, newspapers bleached of print,
Blue plastic-coated wires, styrofoam cups,
A red something, a Christmas ornament.

Flinching, cowlicked, stunned by the six-months' winter,
The grass flushes tawny, deep amethyst,
And keeps its eyes shut to the light.
An alder's leafless crown colours redly.

The landscape, in that old and simple way
Of saying just what happens, "awakens".
It renews itself like the unfolding
Fine linen of stored words heard once a year:

Mary Magdalene and the other Mary
At daybreak on the first day of the week
Came unto that fresh-cut word the sepulchre.
The stone, the vowels sing, was rolled away.

Two men stand by them in shining garments.
He is not here, they say. *He is risen.*
Why seek ye the living among the dead?
Tough-stemmed crocuses stir underfoot.

Envoi

Go little book, *par avion.*
Wing, verses, toward your targets:
Where faces cool and harden behind bars,
Where an idea straps on a pistol,

Where the people eat their right to vote,
Where machine guns and TV cameras
Look from the tops of glass buildings.
Go, little peregrine.

Fly as I taught you
With bombs tucked under your wings,
In a V of attack, low to the ground,
Underneath the enemy's lazy radar.

It's too much though—isn't it, little friend?
You glide over cool marble floors
Out into the womanly moonlight.
A rose vine encircles you, you bleed on the thorns.

Your throat opens to a harmony of seasons.
You sing of the nest, of unruffled June mornings,
Of leaving the nest, of building it again;
Of its perfect circle.

You would have me kill, you whose life is a breath?
I pity you, yes I pity you, you warble,
And take off into the distance
As if you thought you would live forever.

I stand in the predawn field, boots drenched,
The big glove covering my wrist and hand,
And watch you soar, a speck now,
Into the rainy future.

from *The Stonecutter's Hand* (1995)

Xiphias

for Nancy

The fish, the swordfish, *Xiphias gladius* in
Latin, swam deeply in the aquamarine—
Three hundred pounds of nerve, sleek and masterful
In his element.
Our table up the cliff shelved over the scene.

Swordfish was the *plat du jour* that day.
The cook there rubbed it with sea salt,
Garlic, crushed pepper, lemon from the lemon tree,
Kegged olive oil and thyme—
Then grilled it over local hardwood.
It was the best I've ever had.

The ocean depths were the zenith blue
Of our rented Fiat cinquecento.
A schooner skimmed over the lithe warrior in the water.
The harpoonist stretched out shirtless on the bowsprit,
His body one muscle, his arm a coiled rope.

That was before I understood about love.
I knew it would draw me into town over moonlit roads
To spend all my change on one song.
That it would keep me awake all night
And improve how the whippoorwill sang.

I wouldn't have cared if I had driven the Fiat
Off the cliff, so long as we went over together.
You were twenty-two then,
Signorina, in the South of Italy,
And I wished I had packed a gun.

The long shadow swiftly blurred.
The spotter in the crow's nest softly called
In soft Calabrian consonants the lovely word
For fish, which just then thrashed into a school of chub
And filleted a couple of dozen with his sword.

The harpoonist struck.
The three-yard pine shaft blew out for itself a tunnel
Of bubbles and disturbance.
And the blade that fishermen call a "lily"
Jabbed in just behind the gills.

The swordfish spasmed his long body-muscle,
Charged the little dory they had set out,
Stove out a plank or two just above waterline,
And then with the toothed sword jammed in up to his eyes,
The swordfish died.

That fish was lucky. He died there and then.
Pesce spada in Italian.
They lashed the carcass to the schooner,
Tied the wounded dory on behind,
And sailed into harbour.

Aubade

Steam in the pipes.
Birdsong muted.
A prowl of cat.
Ivy on a wall, the breeze layering it,
seen through Venetians.
An arm thrown over the
edge of the bed.

A stocking, a twisted undergarment, shoes.
Empty matchbooks, full ashtrays,
fume of brandy over a glass.

She gets that last twenty
minutes of sleep she likes.
He runs a razor over his jaw,
looking into the steamed mirror in a daze.

Luggage placed by a door.
Some keys on a Queen Anne table.

Savannah, Sleepless

A bell has rung twelve times.
A bell has rung once.
Twice.

Could I be the last non-sleeper in Savannah?
Elevators have been upgathered

And then, with me in one, sent down again
to where duels and steam locomotives
hang on the baize walls.
Billiard balls stand expectantly,
in their round way.

Two people begin to become musical.
Powder-puff, honey-dark skin, pink gown with springy straps,
she can kiss a passing cheek and keep singing.
He tickles the ivories and looks like Nat "King" Cole.
A machine plays the beat for their song.

Two men discuss two women.
Chairs are drawn up.
Names are given.
A notebook sits apart,
entranced by the yin-yang of brandy and cigar.

No, evidently, I am not the last waking human
in the Hilton Hotel.
The singer is explaining she doesn't want
to set the world on fire,
she just wants to start a flame in the heart
of some unspecified "you".

Outside, the million tongues of the city sleep,
and the blue Atlantic draws a breath.

The Winter Funerals

for Mary

The postman totters up our street. He's late
Or early, like spring, or he doesn't come at all.
You practice your violin, I go for a stroll
And watch the oysterman tarring his boat
That the storm stove in—the rough weather that brought
The lines down that night after New Year's
When the farmers' faces ran with tears
Outside the house where Mary Flatley was laid out.

We've brushed our black clothes off and put them away.
Someone is cooking, someone's out tending the stock
In the grainy drizzle that settles the turf smoke.
Obscured up there in the weathered sky,
The wind that troubled our winter still blows above
The village. We drink it at night with our whiskey
And stir it into our morning tea,
Hearing the tune Charlie played over Maggie's grave.

That drowsy reel's feet danced in the new-dug mud
Of the grave, and held its drained face up to the rain
When he played it slow on his dark accordion—
That grievous dance step Charlie played.
It follows me out this morning up and down
As I buy a stamp or run an errand
And go for a pint at Flatley's tavern,
Where Mary's smile is nowhere to be seen.

Nowhere in the pipe smoke and mirrored coolness
Where she heard the farmers' chaff with a tolerant ear.
Nowhere to be seen but present everywhere
Amid the slow talk and the Guinness.
Her smile followed the gossip—predictable
As the stuffed pheasants in their glass cases,
Old as the posters for the Galway races.
She gave a love that was almost invisible—

Like the voice at the foot of the garden, the thorny warble
I hear when I get home and pull on my boots
And squelch out among the cabbages and beets
To spot that spring voice, invisible
Or nearly so, that weightless, redbreasted, sparse-feathered
Heartbeat that lilts in the battered garden,
That sings its song for no sound reason
And dies among the thorns unheralded.

You practise your music, I sniff the wind for a sign,
While down in the mud the cabbages glow
With a green persistence. All day you play
That tune, that same old tune, till it's right as rain.

Rhymes on the Feast of Stephen

Something has gladdened the blankness of this field,
This rectangle pure as the future, bright as a door
Opened onto snowflakes sharpening the air.
Light-syllabled words, words bewilderingly old
Have printed their inky footfalls here.
I hold the piece of paper to the light
And touch with my fingertips the lodged repose
Of music notched into this whiteness of trees.
I pile up winter fuel in the grate,
Then lean back in my chair and breathe a bit.
Nothing to change: This ink is permanent.
I drink the wassail of vowel and consonant.

A Visitation

Why tonight,
  crossing an alien bridge
I should see the faces
  of those two who had died—
damaged moons radiating up
  from the mystery of a river
charging whitely to sea—
  I won't hazard
speculation.
Death is their persuasion, life mine.

One face smashed on the tarmac,
  one face eroded, scabrous,
delirious on hospital sheets.

  Life is the flame that won't singe
anymore
  their danger-prone fingers.

Convergence

You knew it was there, you could sense it
Greenly inherent in the wood
Through dull months when you didn't notice
Life fattening in the bud.
Now April fulfills itself with whitethorn,
And lilacs overarched with birdsong.

A lash under the lid, the suspicion
Of pain in the third molar, a flicker's
Speckled flutter into fieldglasses'
Pursuing circle of focus.
The E-string twists, retrieving, past sharp and flat,
Then sounds the sought-for, in-tune note.

The glow of a summer's day breathing
Off a river at nightfall. Cutlery's faint
Clatter on summer-cottage china
Up-ridge. You cast to a hint
Of trout in a pool. A violent, muscled swirl
And the hard jaw clamps the feathered steel.

What trick of the night's is it, that you wake
Chilled and alert, fingering
A soreness, picturing cells
Gone rife and hungering—
That you know, as the doctor nods you politely
In, what news he has to give you?

Rhyme

A pair of aces. The sound of two hands clapping.
A boy sidearms a flat stone, sailing, skipping
It once, twice, four times over the closed surface
Of water, through air's openness.
The sun's vowel roundly springs from the east
Through throaty birdsong in summer
And vast autumnal drowse of colour,
To rhyme at day's end frosty in the west.

Pepper and salt. The two it takes to tango.
Yin-yang, Fred & Ginger, John & Yoko.
And you yourself this morning, full-sailed, breeze
Into the room where I write, your blouse
Double-rigged, frankly buttoned, billowy—
As if to say rhymes are matched pairs,
Two swayed and balanced, separate spheres,
Two bell-notes, twin poles of discovery.

Over our garden wall, to the top branch
Of the pear tree blossoming now, a bullfinch
Flies. His honed beak businesslike, his burgher's
Stout midsection splendid, he perches
And preens his pink waistcoat. A model of self-esteem.
Then at his side the female alights,
Jostling the fellow as they take their seats,
Banker and wife at the theatre. That's rhyme.

House with Children

for Josh, Julia, Andrew, Charles and Mary

First the white cat named after Indians
Slipped in—too fat by half,
White marked with five black spots like sudden stones
In the snow—poked in through his hidden door,
Set flowing through the house a draft,
A chill tangled in the winter of his fur.

Alerted to those skulks, those leaps, those claws,
The sparkless energy-efficient
Furnace fired, pouring warmth through every vent
Of the house's two-storey stucco repose.

Julia slept her seven summers' worth
On a cloud of goose down, hugged by cushioned paws,
Dreaming. The wind blew out of the north.
Josh sprawled among paper fantasies.
Even Andrew rested from his wonderings,
His pages of lion, witch, and so forth.
Their three doors swayed in the warm domestic breeze
As Iroquois strolled past in his wanderings.

Drawn, was it, by the fragrance of marriage, he leapt
To the bed where the man woke and the woman slept
And the three-years' life between them burned fitfully
In a moment of fever, then woke laughing soundlessly.

Charles woke, and cooled his hands on the cat's chill fur.
In the clock's dimness white and dark spots blended.
The mercury stuck high, snow hung suspended
Like a V of geese over Canada.
The house and its people lodged secure
That night. Snow fell nowhere but Narnia.
There at the back of the wardrobe a door
Between the deep cold and the greatcoats stood ajar.

Table

from the Turkish of Edip Cansever

for Julia

A man filled with the gladness of living
Put his keys on the table,
Put flowers in a copper bowl there.
He put his eggs and milk on the table.
He put there the light that came in through the window,
Sound of a bicycle, sound of a spinning wheel.
The softness of bread and weather he put there.
On the table the man put
Things that happened in his mind.
What he wanted to do in life,
He put that there.
Those he loved, those he didn't love,
The man put them on the table too.
Three times three make nine:
The man put nine on the table.
He was next to the window next to the sky;
He reached out and placed on the table endlessness.
So many days he had wanted to drink a beer!
He put on the table the pouring of that beer.
He placed there his sleep and his wakefulness;
His hunger and his fullness he placed there.

Now that's what I call a table!
It didn't complain at all about the load.
It wobbled once or twice, then stood firm.
The man kept piling things on.

Objects

He would have wrapped a coarse cloth I imagine
About the icon, taking with him the Virgin's
Gaze of power, her countenance blackened
By centuries of candle-blur and worry—
Tucking it away in his saddlebag.
You can see a crease here where the frame was scored
With wire.
        A dim foreknowledge of the road's
Rutted mire and snowdrifts must have shivered
Through his plans as he heard the loud sycamore
Leaves skitter, desiccated, across the bricked
Herringbone of the cloister's footpaths.

Then a sudden whiff of espaliered
Quinces, overripe and unplucked, whets
His sense of loss, the abbey deserted now,
The infidels' bronze mortars thudding closer
Among chestnut trees the order planted
Along their eastern ridges.
        He tenders
Between his hands, before stowing it, the chalice—
Cupping it in his palms the way you hold
A face from your youth, thumbing its silver bowl
Like the cheekbones of the Blessed Virgin.

The hunting glide of a peregrine falcon slices
Through his hesitation. He fumbles the sign of the cross,
Shuts the oak door with an thud behind him,
Then locks it with his medieval key.

And thinking that if God wills, the Emperor's troops
Might fight their way back into these mountains
By spring, he throws the key into a snowdrift
And mounts.

Pasha's Daughter, 1918

in memory of James Stewart-Robinson

Braided into a single complication
Down the back of her nightdress, her hair shows grey
As pearls and white as a cloud as she steps coldly
To open the curtains' plum velvet, stiff with thread of silver,
Onto a sky above Istanbul. Mehmet brings *chai*
On a silver tray worn through to copper.

A Jerusalem cypress in her garden
That arrows the sky as a minaret does—
Its lines liquid as a page of Persian—
A leaded mosque-dome full and silvery in the pause
Between showers, give her the sense of having awakened
And been served tea in Paradise.

Paradise is a bedraggled trapezoid
Of outback, its fountain a brew of leaves,
Its marble paths dog-fouled. The Black Sea wind blows
Trash against untended tulips gone to seed.
Rain storms and gutters down the overarching eaves
And rattles the quiet of her windows.

Tarnished stars invisible above Istanbul
Govern, while trains from Aleppo and the Balkans
Shuttle broken armies home to the capital.
The ground buckles under tombstones. Marble turbans
Crack, as the bones of the ancients are shoveled aside
To make space for the freshly dead.

Mehmet comes in again, six centuries
Of marches and conquests reduced to the dirt
On his cuffs. Moustache dispirited, nomadic cheekbones
Wintry, he lights a fire, smudging the famous skies
With coal scavenged from the cobbled street.
Her eyes would break bones.

Thunder now—like the clatter of musketry.
Like war ponies galloped across borders.
Like bronze siege-cannon pounding Viennese stone.
Like the voice of a shattered gong the circumference of the sky.
"Bring opium to me by the window," she orders,
"While I watch our empire melt in the rain."

Southbound Pullman, 1945

Discharge papers in duffel bags,
Their train thumps half-speed out of Boston.
Sunset kindles the cokey haze
Over Back Bay Station.

Bricky courtyards, windswept corners and
Clotheslines, a view of someone's kitchen.
A Victory garden with fists of cabbage.
Then the lights switch on.

A boy and his father burning leaves,
Obscured by dusk on a patch of green,
Wave up at faces starred in the southbound's
Passing constellation.

Stewards uncork bottles, ice clinks
In the club car. A new deck
Crackles. Atlantic sea-salt blows in,
And a whiff of coalsmoke.

Steam builds. The whistle finds its pitch
And sounds an airy, unstopped note
Over darkling marshes and shore towns
Shutting down for the night.

Dinner is gonged through aisles of opened
Collars and bourbon. The galley
Vents coffee-scald and steak-sizzle
Down the Connecticut Valley.

Penn Station at midnight. Bustle of redcaps,
Morning editions, hot java, trainmen
Tuning the wheels with big wrenches.
Then distances again.

Porterly hands tuck ironed cotton
And turn drowsy blankets back.
Darkness cradles the swaying coaches
Over strumming track.

Snoring. Then a nightmare scream
Jangles to its feet the whole sleeper.
Home voices murmur "You're okay, son."
"The war's over, soldier."

All night the breathing of ploughed fields.
The continent opens like a hand.
Tomorrow, bands and a convertible.
Then fresh mistakes begin.

Five Sketches, Winter

for Kathleen Halme

1.

Bedraggled quadrangle.

A stone sill, chisel-marked.
The snow arranges, flake by flake,
itself over the stone.

2.

The gloom of trees
is a Chinese pistol
Pollocked in ink black shots.

3.

Old copper,
moss-green under shifting white.
Down a steep roof
snow slides.

4.

Vinyl-topped café tables,
one silvery with melting snow,
one still a white loaf

with borders of run.

5.

First snow, then freezing rain.
Down plate glass, a long rattail of drip.

Another plate of cabbage and potatoes, please.

Firstness

Early pleasures please best, some old voice whispers:
Cosy holdings, the heart's iambic thud
And sly wanderings—lip-touchings, long summers,
The rain's pourings and pipings heard from bed.
Earth-smell of old houses, airy ceilings,
A boy's brainy and indolent imaginings.

Twenty years gone then that boy is gone,
Speeding down beach roads in a friend's MG.
Love, or the limey buzz of a g'n't—
Or better, both—and the watery hunter's moon,
Accelerate the engines of the night,
And set a long chase afoot.

Today, twenty years older than that even,
I breathe quietness and fresh-laundered linen,
Kneeling, seeing with eyes opened white brick,
Smelling Sunday, mumbling beside my son those words
About a lost sheep, and someone's having erred.
Thank God for instinct, and beginner's luck.

from *Today in the Café Trieste* (1997)

Today in the Café Trieste

Behind the red lacquered gates,
wine is left to sour, meat to rot.
Outside these gates
lie the bones of the frozen and starved.
The flourishing and the withered
are just a foot apart.
The thought of it is an open wound.
      —Tu Fu, 8th century

The Mountain Goddess, if she is still there,
will see the world all changed.
      —Mao Tse-tung, 1956

Today in the Café Trieste,
      in San Francisco,
I watch through high rippled windows
      flawed and old
the blue sky that reveals
                  and resembles nothing.

A face in the mirror:
   someone else's for an instant
         as I order coffee.
A smile-line cuts the flesh on the left side
         like a scar
   in an otherwise balanced face,
as though everything I've smiled at in thirty-eight years,
            or accepted with irony,
pulled me toward one side of the universe.
My face returns my stare blankly.

117

I slip back into it.
The light slips off my lenses,
    the marine light of the hot afternoon,
                a little too bright for the wine
  I drank last night.

Mrs Giotta says something in Italian:
La vita, life—
    or the world, *il mondo*,
        I think she is saying—
    is a solid, well-made glass.
This Italian lady sets a warm glass
                of something
            in front you,
and you know the world is in order.
When order goes,
glass is the first thing to break.

Mindlessly I watch
    the North Italian daughter-in-law
                open the dishwashing machine
and roll out a tray
    on one-inch plastic wheels—
a tray of dishes like a story
                about the future of the world,
like Buenos Aires' walled-off gardens
            seen from a private plane.
In the upturned tops of green stemware—
        jade lakes, limpid
            half-moons
        of hot water, cooling,
    redolent of jungle spring,
        clean steam rising in the café.

The daughter-in-law
    pumps the espresso machine
like a lady engineer
    in the cab of a steam locomotive
in Italy, after the Revolution.

I sit at my favourite table.

September 9, 1976,
    three years ago,
someone else's paper told me
Mao Tse-tung had died,
    ten minutes into that day.

I sat at this same corner table,
    looking at newsprint photos,
                and watched the sky stream away—
    a wooden flagpole,
a Gothic rooftop wobbly in the old glass.

Five Photographs of Mao Tse-tung

1. WITH CHU TEH IN YENAN, 1937

Mao scowls, a cigarette between his light fingers,
as if he has just inhaled
        and is holding his breath—
no rank on his uniform,
        his feet in cloth slippers.
Chu Teh, his best general, straddles the pavement,
        a broken brick by his sneaker.
Happiness spreads from his peasant eyes.
Mao Tse-tung,
                squinting, high-cheeked, cautious,
seems to be analysing a problem.

2. MAO TSE-TUNG WITH BODYGUARDS,
DURING FLIGHT FROM YENAN, 1948

A character from Chinese opera
— his wife Chiang Ch'ing, "Green River",
                behind him on a shaggy pony—
inconvenienced, merely
                disdainful of enemy bombers,
        their caravan small in the vast landscape.

Tribesmen in the line of march,
    dark Mongolian Bodyguards—
tightness of fear in their faces.

3. Mao Tse-tung in triumph in Beijing, October, 1949

Standing up
in a new jeep with good tyres,
wearing a black, fur-collared, new-looking coat—
      his face turned toward interminable rows
        of motorised artillery,
   freshly painted barrels raised in salute—
Mao's eyes unfocussed into the distance.

4. Beijing, undated

A human face covering the side of a building,
Mao Tse-tung, not so big as the ear
   of his portrait,
silk-suited, surrounded by diplomats and generals,
  stiffly at attention on a balcony
      over the head of his massive image.

Two million people
  in the Place of Heavenly Peace,
holding two million pictures of that face—
as though to answer
the ghosts of all those Mao called
    gentry   landowners
      bourgeois elements,
blood in the river of the Revolution:
How can one say
  that the peasants should not now
rise, and shoot one or two of them
  and bring about
a small-scale reign of terror?

121

A revolution is not
like inviting people to dinner
      or writing an essay,
           or doing fancy needlework. . . .

I remember the XIVth Dalai Lama
   of what is now
"The Autonomous Cultural Region of Tibet"—
in Delhi in the 60s, in exile.
He steps into a taxi
      in monk's robes, with shaved head.
The swarthy, tribal-looking bodyguards
      break off their card game
         and follow him.

"Place on one side,"
  he says to his visitors,
"the dogs of this neighbourhood—
and on the other side, my life.
The lives of the dogs are worth more."

But that day in '76
        I speak of—
everything seemed to rise on one side of life,
      and recede on the other.
I was thirty-five years old.
I ordered a double espresso.
The dust-mottled bust of Dante, now gone,
   glared at me across the bar—
tiring, unresting,
   with his hook nose and predator's eyes.

A newspaper clipping,
San Francisco Chronicle, "The Voice of the West":
"Chinese Radical's Great Leap to Bay Area."

The former Red Guard
stowed away on a boat to Hong Kong . . .
His plaid sofa   his RCA   colour TV,
his view of San Francisco Bay. . . .
An articulate young man,
he has applied to three law schools,
including Harvard . . . .
He has just sold a $160,000 building.

A certain drive, a certain
    assertiveness . . .
as though the Revolution
    equipped him with the tools
to make it
    in America.

The rainbow trout in my daydream
    flashes in glassy water,
snags the wet fly in mid-riffle,
    fights me like a small country.
I play him quiet
    into my quiet hand underwater,
hold him in the current,
    and slip the hook out
        of his hard jaw.

The trout hangs in the current
    as if slow to feel freedom come back
        into his muscles,
    then thrashes free downstream.

Aphorisms of Ancient Sun Tzu,
            5th century BC:
Be as swift as the wind, as secret as the forest,

as consuming as fire, as silent as the mountains,
as impenetrable as darkness, as sudden
as thunderbolts.

War is nothing but lies.

In throwing in troops, drop them
like a millstone on an egg,
the solid on the void.

Mr Giotta turns the café lights on.
It's easy to see
                    the dawn now
             as Chu Teh saw it
when the Long March began:
   Over stones and peaks worn
to slippery smoothness
   by no one knows how many
eons of fierce wind, rains, and snow,
the column of gaunt and ragged
                         men and women,
fleeing Chingkanshan,
   began to creep single-file
along the jagged crest of the
                         mountain spur. . .
By nightfall reached a small
sloping ridge of solid volcanic rock
   where we stopped and ate
      half the cold rice we had brought,
   huddling together and linking arms,
passed the night
      shivering and coughing.

With daybreak they crept like fog
   down an overgrown trail
over the first village:
to drop like a millstone on the enemy garrison—
   "the solid on the void".

           Thousands of rifles and machine-guns
   lay buried on the long trail south . . .
      much ammunition, much machinery,
            much silver.

From a poem by Mao:
I remember how vivid they were
as they gazed upon rivers and mountains:
The Chinese earth gave strength to their words—
and the ancient feudal lords
were something they scraped off their boots.

I look around the café at faces,
   knowing so many.
Ferlinghetti comes in after work,
smiles and frowns at the same time
   as if to say:
   "Where did we meet?"
A student drinks hot chocolate and reads *Dubliners.*

Ten years ago
we fought all day and ran,
   and watched ourselves on network news at night.
The Revolution seemed no farther away
   than squadcar blue-lights whipping
         hypnotically through fuchias
            in the Berkeley hills—
   fear and love in a crowd,

a nose full of teargas,
plate glass heavily smashing.

People say "Our Revolution
   had its effect."
I yawn, and nod in agreement.
But what I see is
"urban guerillas" cleaning houses,
                pumping gas,
cooking eggs at six in the morning
          for someone else,
collecting food stamps,
teaching grammar to convicts,
—revolutionized into poverty—
or invisible in some good job.
"The best minds of my generation" too,
                self-exiled from America,
                       strangers to power,
          a wasted generation.

My teacher from college writes "Alienation
                hovers over your lines
   like the smell of burning flesh
          over the funeral pyres."

I put a dime in the Trieste's jukebox,
          with its unique selection
of Italian arias Greek bouzouki music
          songs in Portuguese from *Black Orpheus*
   thin-air music from the high Andes
          (bass drum and flute).

Maria Callas sings
          "Un Bel Dì Vedremo."
          Silence sinks into the café.

Remember:
The Chinese earth gave strength to their words.

A last photograph:

5. MAO TSE-TUNG SWIMMING THE YANGTSE RIVER,
1966

His solemn, chunky head visible
   above water
      like the head of an old bull—
showing his enemies himself alive,
     Mao floats on his back
  or side-strokes lazily,
   crossing the two-mile river,
  gazing at the changing sky—
oil refineries on the bank,
   mountains in the far distance:

I've just drunk the waters of Changsha,
now I taste fish in the surf at Wuchang.
Let the wind blow, let rain drench me.
I'd rather be here
than wasting time in rooms of power.
Today I am free!
Old Confucius stands on the bank,
                observing:
"All nature is flowing away."

New cars slip through Saturday night—
headlights, red tail-lights streaking,
        rain blowing off the ocean.
I walk through North Beach
   beside and beneath neon bodies

of unreal women.
I light an illegal cigarette
        and smoke it unnoticed through Chinatown
over hosed-down sidewalks smelling of fish,
past the hot windows of Chinese sweatshops
                open to the night—
live pheasants in cages on the roof of a car,
                heads of cattle in buckets,
leopard sharks in shop-windows on beds of ice.

Mah-jong tiles click in below-street parlours.
    Blue light seeps through closed blinds;
red-and-white uniforms swim over TV grass.

Business picks up again at the Golden Dragon,
where blood of seventeen people
        was washed off the floor last year
and the place remodeled.

I gravitate toward my parking place,
    stepping into the baroque church
        of Our Lady of Guadalupe
to shake two junkies who are following me.

In the fragrant semi-darkness
    I touch cool water to my forehead.
The priest hands me pamphlets
    and asks God to bless me.
He stops me as I leave the church
"God bless you," he says the second time.
            "Pray for us all."
I promise to do that, and step outside.
            The two men are gone.

I find the car and drive out past
solid, stone-built Pacific Avenue mansions—
past bars for every kind of drinker—
past everybody and everything there is
                    to buy—
past a Chinese lady in silk
          looking into the vanished sunset—
past the exquisite
three-hundred-year-old military base—
          white markers, thousands
in a forest of mist and cypresses—
out over the Golden Gate
and the spirits of all the dead.
I nudge my car into the northbound stream, alone,
          straight down the middle of the bridge,
into the redwoods and foothills,
into the open darkness.

San Francisco, 1979

from *Six Mile Mountain* (2000)

His Days

When one of his black moods bedevilled him,
When the wince of some remembered pain—
Some wrong done to him, some cruelty of his own—
Hurt him like a surge melting down
Bad wiring, what choice was left him
But to flinch and swallow and bear it like a man?

The cottage's slates and silences became
His kingdom, its weathers his own. He would coax
To a blaze coal and turfs each morning, and chunks
Of beech he split with his own axe.
The farmer's son or Sunday hikers would see him
Hunched at his kitchen table, away in his books.

Then obscurely one morning he'd lock his cottage door.
With a word to no one he'd be gone,
To look at an old church somewhere, or the ruin
Of a tower down a dirt track, or a stone
Incised with markings no one could decipher,
Its language crumbling by degrees in the rain.

He could navigate the old script. And he knew why an arch
Was rounded or gothic. Why the mermaid
Held a mirror. Which sins the monks allowed
Themselves, and which they disavowed.
He knew the griefs of the high kings, belonged to the church
Of bitterness, had bet on the cards of pride.

But when on some grimy market town's main street
He heard a child, eyes widening in wonder,
Call out "Daddy!", reaching for its father,
Or a couple taking snaps of each other;
Then, it seemed, the pain was complete.
The water was wide, and he could not swim over.

A Visit

Mud spattered the windscreen of my rental car.
When I asked where she was buried, a memory fell
Like shade across the face of the woman who lived
In what had been the gate lodge—then a smile,
A shy welcome, and she pointed the way to the churchyard.
Then a child called her, so there was not a soul

Between me and the sand-blasted spire of the Protestant church.
The shape of her headstone, beveled like the gable
Of a Dutch canal-house, was, like her handwriting,
Charactered but unobtrusive. The lichened marble
Put me in mind of the mottled green Parker with which
She used to write. The doll's-house of a school

Stood out from the choir of the church, where Joseph in his coat
Of many colours was first betrayed, where Mary
"Kept all these things and pondered them in her heart".
I peered into those depths, through cobwebbed glass
Where desks swam in the green of a river twilight.
Thumbtacked to the wall was a snapshot of her house,

Gone now, and the print of a Pre-Raphaelite
Madonna and child. My neglect—I had let her grow old!—
Burned in my face, acknowledged now for the first time.
She was Mary in the painting, I was the child—
I could see that now—nurtured and wondered at.
Ungrateful, and leaving already, I had struggled

To step off into an air beyond her containment.
Nothing stirred in that churchyard, or gave the slightest
 impression
Her story and mine impinged on the afternoon.
I turned away, walked back to my car—
Warned off by a treeful of rooks—and drove out the gate.
How long it takes us to become who we are!

Ever

for my mother

And when she was gone
the silver lost its frail brilliance,
the cut glass cobwebbed,
the clocks wound down.

The two brothers
in the story she would read us on Christmas Eve
never made their way in from the blizzard,
never rescued the beggar-woman from the snowdrift
or laid their pennies on the altar,
or found out why the chimes rang.

Father in October

for Brownie and Kate

When the smell of freshly sharpened pencils had lost
Its power to intoxicate, when our first
Infatuation with September had slackened—
With its satchels and homework and new teacher;
When the leaves of the late-blooming chrysanthemums
In our frost-finished back garden had blackened,
One morning my mother would retrieve our winter
Hats and scarves, our gloves and heavy raingear.
My father would go up attic, bring down the storms
And snug them in, between ourselves and the weather.

One hundred years of our family had lived
Beneath that house's airy ceilings, had sat
By a grate where coal sputtered and glowed in the glass
Cases where my grandfather's books were shelved—
Shakespeare, the Brontës, Dickens, Sir Walter Scott.
And the house told stories, of interest only to us:
The well, sealed after Uncle John drowned a cat.
The deep-cut initials my older brother carved
Above the stairs. The bed my mother was born in.
Every dip in the floorboards spoke, every curious stain

Remembered. To marry my mother, my father found
In 1932, was to husband her house.
Its *fin de siècle* wiring was a fireman's nightmare;
What was airy in June was drafty in December.
"Manage", "Simplify", his granite New England

Eyes said. Those Willifords must have seemed another
Species altogether—with their Southernness,
Their leaky roof, their Eastlake furniture.
There was hardly a marble-topped table that didn't wobble,
Or a chair that couldn't have used some glue or a nail.

Saturdays he'd be up by six. First
A shave, and with his shaving brush he'd soap
Clean the lenses of his gold-rimmed glasses.
Then he'd collect himself over coffee and make a list,
Numbered and neat, of his day's projects in the shop
He had built out back under the hickory trees.
A nimbus of sawdust surrounding his concentration,
He'd turn a chair-leg on his lathe, cut out
A bracket or brace with his jigsaw, then fashion
A toy pistol for me, or a paddle-wheel boat.

Daddy's real work was engineering. His own
Dreams and epiphanies came to him, I imagine,
In the language of his calling—straightedged and clear
As a blueprint, verifiable by time and motion
Studies. His few inventions that made a profit,
The many he drew in his mind but had to give
Up on, lived a life pristine and platonic—
Not subject to half-measures or the change of season,
Not battered by weather or in need of repair
Like the mortal house I judged him master of.

Rain

The rain, the incessant drench,
    the lap of it puddling up,
       seen through spattered window-glass.
And all of us in that long house together
    where all the talk was of the weather,
   house-partying on a rainy weekend.

Fragrance of toast, incessant cups of tea.
The wind mulled and hovered,
   the wind set all the buttercups in the field a-tremble.
I would sit all morning in the blue armchair transfixed,
     hearing the whoosh and settle of wind and rain
    surround and define
      the astral shape of the cottage.

The rain was sleep till half past ten,
the rain was not having to shave,
the rain was opium,
the rain was an ocean voyage through blackness.
The rain was a whisper under coverlets,
   a barely moving lace between ourselves and the trees.
The rain was constant, sempiternal, older than woodsmoke.

And then it would bow its head and subside,
   and a blackbird
tuning cleanly pinnacles of delight from a dry perch
      under dripping boughs
would put you in mind
of Noah and his lot
    drifting becalmed when the waters retreated.

I wanted it never to end.
I wanted to deconstitute and emanate out
                beyond the force-field of the cottage
          like lamplight through wet windows,
                    and let the rain possess me entirely—
          let it soak right down
                into the pores of my happiness.

The World Is

The world is a man with big hands
and a mouth full of teeth.
The world is a ton of bricks, a busy signal,
your contempt for my small talk.
It's the crispy lace that hardens
around the egg you fry each morning
sunny side up.

The world is the last week of August,
the fumes that dizzy up into the heat
when you fill your tank
on the way to work late, again.
The world is "Please take a seat over there."
The world is "It'll have to come out."
The world is "Have a nice day."

The world is "What is that peculiar smell?"
The world is the button that popped off,
the watch that stopped, the lump you discover and turn on
        the light.
The world is a full ashtray, the world is that grey look,
the world is the County Coroner of Shelby County.
The world is a cortège of limousines,
an old man edging the grass from around a stone.

The world is "Ulster Says No!", the world is reliable
sources, a loud bang and shattered glass raining down on
        shoppers.
The world is a severed arm in a box of cabbages, "And then
the second bomb went off and we didn't know which
way to run." The world is Semtex and black balaclavas
and mouth-to-mouth resuscitation. The world is
car alarms silenced, and a street suddenly empty.

The world is one thousand dead today in the camps.
The world is sixty thousand latrines, the world is
bulldozers pushing bodies and parts of bodies into a ditch.
The world is dysentery and cholera,
infected blood, and vomit.
The world is mortality rates, and rape as an instrument of war.
        The world
is a 12-year-old with a Walkman, a can of Coke, and an Uzi.

The Alley Behind Ocean Drive

On beach sand two thousand footprints
Cross and overlay
And form or seem to form a pattern.
Girls speaking Italian
Take off their tops
And breathe the sun in through their pores.

The sun sets gorgeously
And then the *jeunesse dorée*, or
Eurotrash as they are called locally,
Drift back to their suites to change.
Then they emanate out onto Ocean Drive,
Sherbet-coloured, to please the night air.

Behind Ocean Drive and the Colony Hotel
Runs an alley, unnamed,
Where Cuba comes to work.
When someone in the grill orders in English
The dishes get shouted
Out through the kitchen in Spanish.

People come here from far away
To spend money. Behind the Imperial,
In the alley, someone chops ice, fish are gutted,
Dirt gets washed off roots.
The ditch that runs down the
Middle of it runs red.

Out on Ocean the guy with the parrot angles for tips,
Madame Amnesia deals out a Tarot hand,
Iguana-on-a-bicycle lady wobbles
Amongst the Eurotrash. I write
My page, my way is paid.
All of us ride the swell of a tide.

The offal, the scales, the T-bones from steaks,
The hearts and lemon rinds, are put in bags
That the city comes by and collects.
Two towels hang on a balcony overlooking the alley.
A man in a white apron
Stands outside alone and smokes.

My Father's Glen Plaid Jacket

That bias-cut seam around the collar
has come unstitched now.
The label says Oak Hall, Memphis.
Its oak clusters evoke
a banqueting hall and woodsmoke of Englishness.
But it's my Dad's jacket.
His sweat must still be somewhere in the satin lining.

I wear the thousand times he put it on
to drink old-fashioneds,
or to go to the theatre,
and I can see him in it at the railing
as some bargain cruise ship left for South America.
But mostly when he put it on to go to church.

I wear it and try to be true
and oaklike, as he was,
knowing that while God's kingdom
might come
and His will might be done
on earth as it is in Heaven—
whether or not we can quite follow it—,

as for the likes of my father and me, we
sweated in a white collar for our daily bread
and tried to live within the boundaries
set by our trespasses,
asking not to be led into temptation—

working, putting money in the bank,
kneeling to pray
while unceasingly, mysteriously
moved around us
the kingdom, the power, the glory.

The Emigrant

Two places only
there were:
here and America.
The four corners of the farm,
and gone-beyond-the-sea.

With a twopenny nail
he etched into the iron
shank of his spade
the word "Destiny",
drove it with his boot smartly into the earth
and left it standing.

Abroad commenced
at the town line.
The New World blinded him
on the Navan road
and again the first time he tried to speak English
and again the first time he saw an orange.

Anaesthetised by reels and barrels of porter
and eight renditions of "The Parting Glass",
he fell asleep to the groan of oars
and awoke to a diesel thrust
and sleet over mountainous seas.

Am I Like a Tree

planted by the water
in this congregation, in my father's glen plaid jacket?
What are these other
well-dressed communicants doing here?

My camel would balk at any attempt
to drive him through the eye of a needle.
What good would it do
to abandon my father and my mother,
now both gone anyway,
and give my worldly goods to be sold?

Yet I think I know what it means
to take up my cross daily.

What am I to make of this advice
to seek first the kingdom of Heaven?
The paths of righteousness
are brambled over, are they not?—
rocky, and the footing is bad.

Yet even I have sat down among stones
rough-hewn into blocks two cubits on a side,
and counted my money out in my hands
to see if I could pay to have my tower built.

Asters, I think it is,
on the altar. Someone has laundered and starched the cloth
and now it reflects whitely up onto the silver chalice
as I would expect it to do
at a luncheon in Heaven.

Though I may join my voice with angels and archangels
and with all the company of Heaven, evermore praising
Thee and singing this hymn to proclaim the glory
of Thy name,
and though I may even be allowed sometimes
to drink the cup of salvation
and eat the bread of Heaven,
I could never really cut it
as a disciple.

Step sure-footedly.
Be a tree with roots.
Have money in your hand.
Kneel. Rejoice.

We all know one fine morning
we will be called on
in one breath
to renounce all that we have.

Petition

I was taught as a child about the kingdom
And the power, and the glory that overarches
Our little lives. And when my hard moment came,
I prayed—that surely is the word—"Let me live".
I breathed that prayer out into a kindly sensate
Surround I could feel, a power I could touch,
If only in thought: an essence of the air
I breathed, which somehow cared for me, whether
I believed or understood—that wasn't the point.
"Let me live. Please. I have work to do."

When I thought "kingdom" I pictured a messenger,
The hooves of his ready pony pounding stones
Across a riverbed. A night of frost
And alarms. Under black pines, iron gates opened
To the king's hunting lodge up a mountain,
Letters to the court in his saddlebags,
My petition only one of many.
But it would be entered in the big ledger
And attended to in good time. I could picture
The broad nib of the scribe's pen scoring the fibre
Of the paper. "Let me live" was my petition,
"I have people who depend on me."

Glory I knew little about firsthand—
A high-raftered hall with a thousand beeswax candles
Blazing, glimpsed through mullioned windows.
I stood outside in the snow looking up
While the hard, faithful little fist of muscle
Inside my chest opened and closed, hammered
And hesitated, skipped and fluttered, praying.

Six Mile Mountain

The ground held more stones than dirt. No arrowheads,
No shaped flint-chips rose to their pick and shovel.
No one had disturbed these rocks since God and the glacier
Laid them down in anger.

Dogwood misted the woods, forsythia brightened.
The stores in Six Mile were selling flowers for Easter.
They attacked the shelved-in limestone with their pick,
And flecks rained dryly down on dead oak leaves.

Tears fell into the hole they were digging.
They sweated out last night's whiskey and grief.
In the high air's stillness that hard metallic ping
Ricocheted off tree trunks, bare and obdurate.

Finally the earth's coolness breathed up to them.
Little winged things flitted in the air above
The grave. Thumbnail-sized black butterflies appeared.
Black-capped chickadees perched on the black limbs

And answered the sharpened cries of pick and shovel.
The day warmed. Mare's-tails flared across the sky's
Bland cerulean. In the air-drifts
That skimmed the ridge a hawk glided, watching.

The Button

for Áine and Jeff O'Connell

That button dangled,
threadwork of a spider
who has flunked her Home Ec. course.
My jacket, already a size too loose,
lagged off one shoulder
as if blown by an August wind.

Needle and thread I needed, sharpness
and extension, penetration and follow-through.
First bought a black pig-snout of a spool.
Then Sarah looked in the kitchen and found
in the third drawer down, her mother's needle—
unbending, a fairy pikestaff.

Outdoors, while swallows and house martins swooped
near enough to tell them apart—
treble twitter of the swallow from the dull "stirrup"
of the martin—I poked, slow-fingered seamster,
the snub needle nose through corduroy
and secured that errant discus of bone.

Then put the jacket on again,
drew together the two halves of my person,
fastened that essential button,
and walked off into what awaited.

Incident

I slept, dead to the world, then awoke.
My daughter stood at the foot of the bed
calling me to dinner, her corn-stubble hair
dyed red in the sunset. The honest wells
of her eyes brimmed toward me. I was grateful.
My sleep had been summery and boatlike.

Nothing had stopped. My sheets were not marble,
the earthy savour of death did not surround me.
All it was, was a June evening and time
for dinner. I lay in bed a moment longer
and studied the lifeline on my palm,
how it cut passionately into the flesh,
then jagged abruptly to one side
like a slantwise heartbeat.

I was dead no longer. I had come back
from that slow place, that backward-flowing river,
that acre of reticence. Now I had eyes
once more to see and perceive in this world.
It was "Hi, honey", "Hi, Dad", and "How was your nap?"—
corn on the cob and salad from the garden
and coffee in my favourite cup.

Exilium

The imperial city toward which all roads tend,
Which codifies the laws and dispatches them
By runner or fax to expectant provinces
This is not. It's an improvised mélange
Mushrooming along the banks of a tidal river,
Suffering the moods of its irrational weather
And a population with much to complain about.

Though you could dignify what draws you here
By calling it exile, your solitude is your choice,
Even when it racks you, even when
Your tendons stretch with what you have to carry.
Out you go tonight making the rounds, mapping
A route through the city's drizzly melancholia
Down streets of broad colonial emptiness.

Step inside a stained glass door or two
Where shag and porter cloud the conversation.
Sip a slow pint in the company of strangers
While outside the rain slurs through globed lamp-glow.
The evening ages. A notebook fills with your
Idiosyncratic alphabet. Then the pubs close.

The pubs close, the streets rain-slick and desultory.
A cafeteria then—everybody's
Hangout, where plain lives put in appearances
Over tea and a bun. The cash register whirrs,
The steamy rush of the coffee machine backgrounds
A clink of ironstone plates and stainless steel.

No sign of leisure here: every life
In the room carries the imprint of having worked
The livelong day—not to boast or prove
A point, but simply because what else is there?

The way an old sufferer, grey hair wispy and thin,
Handles her knife, addressing a plate of fish,
Reaches you, touches some common chord.
Despite what they say about you—beyond your remoteness,
Your severe judgments on your fellow creatures—
You've some connection still to the human race.
Hypercritical, incommunicado,
It's good to know deep down you're one of us.

We Kept Missing Each Other

Those nights I anchored the far end
of the bar at the Black Mariah,
      spilling drinks and feeding
            the jukebox with lugubrious quarters,
you'd be halfway up Mount Analogue
hooded in that weird white kaftan of yours,
sitting in the lotus mumbling your incomprehensible mantra,
inhaling moonlight through the business end of your kundalini.

But when I tried to join you, belaying up
a rubble-choked crevasse—
my knuckles bleeding, one knee out of whack—
I found the hut empty,
your devotional candle still a-smoulder.
Years later I heard you had something going on Wall Street,
were getting pretty good at puts and takes.

Myself, I was always shy around girls.
          You had if anything too many of them.
"A thirst for loving shook him like a snake," they quoted.
Porfirio Rubirosa just didn't measure up, they said.
The word Fred Astaire was mentioned.

      We kept missing each other.
I was living on a commune in Venezuela
shrimp-fishing off a houseboat
drift-fishing for sharks.
         You were cultivating the perfect lawn.
Your garage was in perfect order.
The wax job on your Buick was dazzling.

I paid off my debts, got a job
writing for *The Wall Street Journal.*
My rental properties were starting to pay off.
That's when I found you working as a shade-tree mechanic
                                        outside Yuma, Arizona.
Brought you a six-pack of Pabst Blue Ribbon while you
rebuilt a Volkswagen engine on a riverbank under cottonwoods.

                    I felt most at ease in a hotel,
liked putting my belongings into impersonal drawers.
    You were spending most of your time at home by this point,
smoking your pipe by the fire looking Victorian,
a paterfamilias surrounded by the next generation.

Just to think that Richard was your name too!

Uncollected Poems (2001—2007)

The Nest

The building of it took place right under our noses,
in the hedge that bordered our lives just off our porch.
So at first we missed it, busy about our own
arrivals and departures, till the nest was good to go:
a springy wicker hold-all fitted into the notch
where branches diverged like the ribs of a vaulted arch
in a chapel that sways with all breezes
that blow, gets soaked in every rain.

Those cardinals with their blurred red
flourishes, scarlet avatars of pure instinct
coming and going with twigs in their beaks. Next
three eggs, and the female brooding on her nest
like a feathery smooth boat at drydock,
like a china hen in a farmhouse kitchen.
Then three crowded skyward mouths, pure need,
three dowdy tulips gaping toward the sun.

But a day came when they were gone for good
and we were not around to see—
after weeks when they were the talk of our household:
nest built, eggs laid, chicks hatched and flown
past the porch and trellis and into the open sky,
leaving the two of us here on our own,
peering down into their derelict oval.
I never saw anything so empty.

A House in the Country

in memory of George MacBeth

Books, poets, talk, a room full of cigarette smoke—
Slow drains, power erratic since lightning struck
The house on Midsummer's Eve. A traveller through
These parts by night, his headlights slicing hedgerow,
Limestone wall and bog, might startle at the blaze
Of windowed candles high up through beech trees.

A mélange of languages, well-chosen malice,
The unyoked humour of our idleness—
Gossip, aesthetics, three or four bottles of red;
More of the same, then everyone's off to bed
Down unsteady corridors, our host's words ringing
In our ears as we pack it in: "If you need anything,
Just scream."

        A conversation in the shape of a table
Devolves now into twelve individual
Selves. A woman undresses and reads a novel.
Outside, a dog barks. A clock ticks on a shelf.
A man reviewing the day reproaches himself.
Now the boards and beams of the house relax,
And a well-constructed accent deconstructs
In the voiceless speech of dreams. Curtains of rain

Blow in. The great square mass of limestone,
Its high-pitched windows extinguished one by one,
Lets slip the ropes that kept night moored to day
And floats down the estuary of the Milky Way.

Once

It pours out, the summer.
      This morning we woke cold
on the sleeping porch, smelling woodsmoke.
I dreamed that the poker-faced jacks and queens and kings
from our low-stakes summer games stepped
               out of their one-dimensionality
and slashed at each other with cardboard swords.

The summer drains away somewhere
inside the hard inner tissue of trees.
The island in midstream—grassy, wildflowery—
dries imperceptibly to a patch of straw.

It's goodbye to the list that begins "a pair"
       and ends "straight flush",
goodbye to the bird book and the
            Book of Michigan Wildflowers
and the book of stars.
Goodbye to the moon that inflamed
       the crazy pack-music of coyotes.

Goodbye to the rough-legged hawk, and the branch he lit on
across the river our last morning;
my effort to hold completely still
while I brought the field glasses into
       focus on his beak,
and his eyes like twin vendettas;
the night four fives beat a royal straight in the last hand—
       those moments
               are absorbed
into a recapitulation called "yesterday",

163

"last week", "last month", "last summer",
becoming at last a birdlike speck inside the cloud
        that sails massively away behind us—

a glimmer, something unplaceable,
a brushstroke of sunlight on a screen
        in the memory of one of our children
from a time we lived happy in the full day.

The barred owl in the woods on the other
        bank of the river called,
and I heard his flourish of eight notes in the dark
for the first time in my life,
        and maybe never again.

Those clouds this morning that mount
        stratum by stratum higher
behind a wind out of Canada
will never configure themselves the same
        way again, ever.

Our dreams, the hands that were dealt us,
wherever it was the hawk's
        hunt took him that August morning,
whatever drew the owl into earshot that midnight—
none of this will repeat.

Everything only happens once.

Ars Poetica

Brush from my heart
the fine particulate matter of the World
Trade Center.
What's left of it floating
still in the air we breathe
keeps us from thinking straight.

Revive me now
with anything low-tech, homemade,
handwoven from living fibers,
written with a fountain pen.

Show me lacquered Chinese red
of a box with three lucky coins in it,
thumbed turquoise of Tibetan
prayer beads hidden from soldiers—
even the powder-blue, tragic, compromised star,
six-pointed on a field of white,
flying over a tank that grinds down on Bethlehem.

Lift my eyes to the disk of the midday sun
seen through clouds
where our towers stood.

Slow me down for once in my life
to the gait of a camel crossing from
        Peshawar to Khandahar
with bags of rice strapped to its saddle,
while the camel driver cranes up
over his shoulder at the
vapour trails of a B52.

Show me struck flint of the North Star,
big splayed kite-frame of the Southern Cross,
and ask me to imagine how they look
from the Southern hemisphere—
while the beggar-man with his load of kindling
crosses the moon people see from China.

Write your words out Yankee-plain
and iconic as the Roman numerals
printed on the face of the clock
that kept time in my mother's kitchen.
Maybe that hand-wound pulse
will stop me thinking about
the NASDAQ, smiley faces, CEOs,
television, and Global Positioning Systems

guiding democracy bombs
into wars where people on the ground
shelter in tarpaper
shacks under roofs of corrugated tin
or pick their way maimed through mine-fields
trying to reach their olive groves.

I too love the primary colours of the flag—
its classic red and white stripes,
its machine-sewn stars
spangled over a field of blue
breezing in the September sky
this day of days.

But I've had it with "God Bless America".
Let blessings fall wherever there is need for them.
My country, it's not just
'tis of thee I sing.

When the "inevitable clash
of civilizations" crowd gets cranked up,
help me contemplate harmony.
Play me the world's music.
Let human fingers pluck the strings of
instruments fashioned from living forests.

Speak to me
in the wavery melismas of the call to prayer
that a billion people hear
this morning from a minaret before dawn,

while I feel in my bones
the bronze reverberations
of a bell that memorialises all we have lost.

1 January 2002

from *The New Life* (2008)

The New Life

dawns obscurely one morning
as you wake.
Pale light
gives a lick of white
to the woodwork framing a north-facing window.

It begins as imperceptibly
as the sound of a fountain pen
filling with fresh ink.

The new life
means deciding to leave,
shaving your head,
putting your things into two shopping bags
and getting on a bus.

The bare spot on your ring finger
reddens in the sun.

In the new life you wake up under a bridge
and light two cigarettes
off a single match—
one for your companion,
one for yourself.

Meeting on the Turret Stairs

"Lie down beside me," I whispered.
So we lay on the bed
in that room that was the whole world to us.
Outside, the innkeeper's children
kicked a soccer ball along the quay.
Seagulls flocked and dispersed,
and the busy foolish world went about its foolish business.

I shut my eyes and
we met on turret stairs.
I felt the braid of your hair
brush my cheek like a glance.
In the distance someone was blowing a horn.
Voices, and boots hurrying across the boards overhead
as the tower awoke by torchlight.

I opened my eyes then and saw
you watching me from the pillow,
your agate eyes two demi-lunettes.
Horses neighed in the place I was coming out of,
and stamped their iron-shod hooves
on the stones of the stable yard below,
striking sparks like the flinty stars.
A banner snapped in the sharp breeze
as dawn blazed through.
I could smell a river close by,
your body opening to my hands.

How the Day Began

to Grace

Step by step the muezzin climbed
the hundred-and-one steps of his minaret
and assaulted the dark streets with the majesty of God.
His notes floated like jellyfish of the voice,
like the breasts of a woman
as she rides above a man,

then hardened when they struck the city's stone facades.
The street dogs roused. They took it into their heads
to rival the call to prayer with their howling.
That woke the crows, who grumbled in their leathery language
and flapped their wings like an ancient grudge
and woke the seagulls, who flocked and glided,
bringing whiteness to the city grey with dawn.

So now there were three colours:
Black of crows' wings stretching back to a time
before there was such a thing as time.
Grey of dawn and limestone and the lungs of old men
as they crept down city streets to pray in the mosque.
White of sea breeze and seagulls' ascension,
and white of the sheets where we woke.

Down in the mosque the old men had washed
away the night's blackness and were bending to their prayers,
stroking their grey beards and mumbling over their beads.
The dogs trotted along the pavement
and woke the sparrows, who told the air it was truly day.

A white tomcat named Nero curled around a juniper bush
in a flowerpot, then grumped and stretched and yawned,
and watched with sleepy eyes the sparrows' doings.

And then what happened, darling?
You sidled alongside the length of my body
and we went back to sleep for awhile.
From down in the street I heard two clangs of a trolley bell
and the surge of shopfront shutters yanked open,
and the steamy rush of a coffee machine.
You backed up onto me and warmed my hand on your breast.
What country were we in? Who was God? I couldn't remember.
The air smelled of everything.

They Gambled for Your Clothes

Even with your head so wrong,
so eggshell-fragile,
nerve endings strobing out of control,
somehow here you are,
and for the moment nothing hurts.

Fight to stay awake and follow
her hands, skill of her fingers as she undoes
your bootlaces, works the boots off
your stiffened feet
and laves them—
silver bracelets on her wrists—
in the flinty stream
that runs through her property.

The dead skin of your ankles
shrieks morbidly,
blue and livid.

What a salad she has prepared for you—
what stainy walnuts,
what bitter curly greens veined
hallucinatory red.

She has found your hat somewhere in the road
and smoothed the dents away,
the bits of broken glass.
There your denim jacket is,
artfully mended, the blood washed out of it.

Amulets

Everything's all wrong today, my love.
I must have forgotten
to bow to the new moon
when she rose.

I'll go down on my hands and knees
and search in the gravel for five smooth stones,
each one different,
then knot them together
on a blood-red string
and hang them over our bed
to keep away nightmares.

Poor as my needle skills are,
I'll sew a jacket of red flannel
over a horseshoe
and keep it under the mattress,
tie a skeleton key to a bit of rope
to ward off the horrors.

Make me a pin cushion in the shape of a domino
marked with seven lucky dots.
Send down to the butcher shop
for a cow's head and a twisty ram's-horn
to ward off lightning strikes.

Give me one of your dance pumps
will you darling,
from your party days?
I'll spray-paint it gold
and put it on the mantelpiece
to bring good luck down our chimney.

Look at it glistening there in the moonlight!

Cabbage

You planted cabbages to please me,
I know.
And there the last three or four of them clung
like pock-marked green moons in orbit
across the muddy sky of the garden slope.

We had to get out the hatchet
to chop the woody stem off the one I wanted.
And then I pulled off leaf after leaf,
each rubbery jacket bull's-eyed
like cigarette burns on an unfortunate table,
where slugs had tried to burrow in.

Before I brought it inside for a good scrub
I hacked off
half-a-dozen leaves with my pocket knife
and flung them onto the compost heap,
flicking slugs off,
lacking the zeal even to deprive
them of their disgusting lives.
Autumn is here, and where
is the gardener's thoroughness
that would have been mine in March or May?

The essence of cabbage
as I chopped through its crunchy thickness
on the kitchen counter
was what the word October
smells like.

The pure white-and-greenness
that filled my head
with what grows and keeps on growing
was what I had needed all this
short and getting-shorter day.

How to Get There

Take the old road out of town.
Follow it
to where crabgrass snaggles up
through cracks in the concrete
and the day turns chilly.
The sky you thought
roofed summer and a lake,
picnics and the breast stroke and an Indigo
Bunting poised on the finial of a jack pine
contains, instead, Canada as seen on weather radar—
flurries, and an air-blast
from shores where ice-floes crumble off a glacier.

Bear south when you spot
a pillar of cumulus stacked up in the heartbreaking
dense blue above a bungalow where
a man and a woman in canvas lawn chairs
sit with their backs turned to each other,
and a tow-headed kid
manoeuvres a nicked yellow toy dump truck
through a canyon ten inches deep,
while black ants observe.

Don't stop. You can't stop. Keep going
until you reach an intersection
where thunder percusses the shuddering inner spaces of sky
and lightens from within
cloud-pockets going dove-grey and gun-metal blue—

past a '48 straight-eight Buick
and thumb-sucking and daydreams,
past words like destination, and hot and cold,
and shame and regret
and starry diadem and Old Town canoe.

Keep driving
through the gap that opens between two novice heartbeats.
Before decades, before skies, before the first summer,
before any knowledge of roads and weather.
Back to where you are an infant again, open-mouthed,
and the whole world lies in wait for your wondering eyes.

Watcher Over the Dead

in memoriam A.N.L., 1902-1995

I left the brandy and the flushed faces and the stories and tears at
      the wake,
recalling the time
we sat around the fire in his log house in Monteagle, drinking
      Old Weller's from silver julep cups,
and he insisted we read aloud
from a newspaper story that described him at seventy-five
as "barrel-chested and sexy".
He crowed when we got to that part.

Not even my old friends would have understood if I tried to tell
      them
how he anointed my house with fire
six hundred miles away on the night of the funeral
when a candle in his namesake my son Andrew's room burned
      out of control—
imperilling all but injuring no one.

But that hadn't happened yet, wasn't going
to happen till after his body went into the ground—
and I'm not sure if I have understood that mystery yet.

I left the wake and walked out under oak leaves and the round
      moon
along the top of the mountain to the chapel of St. Augustine.
It was three in the morning.
The hour struck, and that reverberation of bronze and stone
touched the depths at which his death was lodged in my being.

Up in the west wall the rose window glowed
rose-madder and scarlet and some blue I can't render.
The carpenter wasn't ready yet with the coffin lid
which the next day in our dark suits we took turns
shovelling the gravelly red dirt onto.
So only a cloth stretched over the open box standing on trestles
        that night.
I lifted it, and there was the man I had known.

His eyes were shut. His face clenched around some preoccupation
that made him seem not himself at all—
he who was arch and merry, and delighted in mimicry.

I touched his heavy hands with their ridged fingernails.
I touched his cheek—hard as plaster, colder than anything that
        lives.
Again the tower clockworks ground into motion.

First It Is Taken Away from Me

And now I am home again.
I can sit out in my pyjama bottoms,
                        two cats sprawled
belly-down on the warm deckboards
                        to converse with
the Saturday after Father's Day.
The air is saturated with moisture
as a rum cake is with rum.

Like a tourist, like a slow boater,
                        like a firefly past the solstice,
I hover and scull and wobble
through these haunts and currents and air-pockets—
the day's emptiness
              radiant in the hollow of my spine.

Of the hospital I remember only:
Dry mouth, icy feet, rough dreams.
Nausea of waxed linoleum
down a hall the gurney ran along
                        at scaresome speed.
The gabble of television sets,
and low voices leaking through half-closed doors.
The graph of the monitor repeated, repeated, repeated.

Burgundy velvet like the robe of a grand vizier,
the clematis blossoms like big sagging stars
                                    or moonfish
soak light in and collapse it into their mystery.

The clematis plays Juliet on her balcony,
bosoming out into moonlight,
ripe with the desire to be known,
giving herself, wishing to taste and be
permeated by the world,
        as if she had never breathed air till now.

That's how it is with me,
                wing-shot and hampered as I am,
idly rubbing the IV tape marks off my arm.

First it is taken away from me,
then it is given back.

One Morning a Rose Blooms

and swallows glide atop heat-swells.
You gaze up at the black walnut tree
over the deck as if it would never alter.

But all at once the leaves have gone yellow.
Then one morning the tree is a bleak crown;
tweeds and flannels hang in your closet.

Another morning you are looking for your gloves
and the phone number
of the man you buy firewood from.

The deck has been cleared now and swept clean.
A crow tries to fly but the wind blows him sideways
in its relentlessness.

How good to have built a sanctuary
and put a roof on it—
painted it green and awakened a fire

at the heart of it to splinter the distances
between this room and the cold
miles of the galaxies.

Flowers, because everyone needs
the transport of flowers to take away
the marks made on the heart by treachery

and blandness and stupidity—
your own as much as others'.
That's what darkness is.

The sky goes blank for an afternoon
and a morning. Then it rains.
And then the snow starts to fall.

This is why you have brought a tree inside
and put lights on it
and filled your house with

fragrance and fire and food and
carols for Christmas morning:
Noel, Noel, Noel.

Arrival

to Mary

Remember how knackered we were,
                    how wobbly at the ankles—
burning ourselves out on the road,
                    knocking on Heaven's door?
Exhaustion was part of our intoxication—
          exhaustion, repairs, Bob Dylan,
                    uncertain breakfasts, highway miles.

We turned our wheels in toward the curb,
          detritus of the journey adrift around our feet,
and stumbled out of
                    the truck heavy with our East Coast belongings,
onto the legendary streets of Denver,
          its sky streaked apple-green at dawn—

you in your sheepskin coat,
                    me in my halo of anticipation,
the children loosed from their car-seat and crib
                    blinking at arrival and
          brick storefront fantasias emerging from the darkness,
coalsmoke in our wintry nostrils.

          In our retinas, a sky adorned with clouds
                    forever regrouped ahead of us.
Rubber-banded to the sun-visor,
                    an interstate map of the US
          spanned the hemisphere's curve
                              from Boston to the Rockies.

Sure, we could have made a
            more elegant appearance—
I could even have shaved off my road-stubble.

Yet here we were
                emerging from the tunnel of distance, a family.
Somehow you had entrusted your future
            to my hands on the wheel and my foot on the gas,
my skill with a screwdriver and socket-wrench and fountain pen,
                my blood in the veins of your babies.

In the Parking Lot of the Muffler Shop

for Gary Snyder and Keith Taylor

Between the muffler shop and the Shell station
three pines that survive where four were planted
on a strip of earth five feet across, forty long,
spill their seed cones out onto asphalt.
The pungency of eight stunted junipers
quickens the lunchtime air.

I kick indifferently among
the jetsam that has sedimented up
against the curb somebody
once painted white and then forgot about.
Dandelions take root in black sand
among filter tips, pine needles,
the snapped-off bottleneck from a longneck Bud,
rust and rubber of

manufactured parts that made cars go and stop,
things that appeased the snarl of engines
and spread the pollution out evenly.

Cool air smelling of tyres and gear-box oil
exhales from the service bay of the muffler shop
as from a mountain cave.
Inside, the measured clank of heavy tools
applied with deliberation.

Three trees don't make a forest.
I sit in the shade of this reservation
between a white Cadillac and a red pine,

and a voice says to me:
Archaeologise the ordinary.
Sing songs about the late Machine Age.
Chronicle the in-between.

In the vacancy of noon,
sparrows twitter. At a distance, a phone rings.
Right here where they have spent the whole of their lives,
three pines stand.

Istanbul: Meditations on Empire

for Clifford Endres

The poem I wrote last night in my dream
disappears before breakfast.
Scraps of it blow by me
down thousand-year-old streets:
Centurions on the march,
columns of legions
with faces identically carved, spears at the ready.
And out in front of them, warrior emperors
with archangelic profiles and hawk-like zealots' eyes.
In winged boots of silver they strode,
crosses on their banners.
Seraphic script told their legends in Greek.

St. Gregory of Nyssa writes: *I wish to know*
the price of bread. The bread man answers,
"The Father is greater than the son." I ask whether my
bath is ready. My servant replies,
"The son has been made from nothing."
In streets, markets, squares and crossroads,
they talk of nothing else.
When they deposed an emperor, they would slit his tongue
and cut off his nose.

Plastic bottles, filter tips
and every other non-biodegradable thing
piles up around
rows of helmeted marble legions
stuck haphazardly in the mud

beside a bus stop and a mosque
after the archaeologists left.
Among the huge peacock-eyes on fallen marble shafts
one row of soldiers has been cemented in upside down.

It's all use and re-use and refuse.
Bells from my dream hammer against
the cracked and buckled marble of Byzantium.
God rings the bells, earth rings the bells, the sky itself is ringing.
The Holy Wisdom, the Great Church, is ringing out the message.
For every bell there is a priest, and for every priest a deacon.
To the left the emperor is singing, to the right the patriarch,
and all the columns tremble with the thunder of the chant
while nomadic border-fighters, their eyes blood-inflamed,
muscle over the city walls
and their cannons blast gaps through which more fighters pour.

Once Constantine's city was looted and ravished
for the customary three days
and the fires died down—
while stiffening corpses lay about the streets
and dogs fattened,
the Conqueror, in sky-blue boots,
wearing an enormous turban,
dismounted, sprinkling a handful of dust on his head,
and entered through one of the church's nine bronze doors,
quoting a melancholy distich in Persian—
something about a spider
spinning her web in the Palace of the Caesars
and an owl hooting from the towers
of a king whose name I don't remember.

Dome over dome over dome
gone the way the Venetians would go
with their glorious waterborne empire.
The polluted tides of history slosh up underneath it all—
the stone lion of St Mark's propping up
an eroded tablet of Christ's gospel
at high tide
of oil-slicks and bitter coffee and coal smoke
in any port on the Mediterranean
from Malta to Constantinople.

I make my way with a headache
and unsure feet down a steep street in Pera
where a dead-drunk woman in a cotton house dress
lies passed out on the sidewalk,
everyone just walking around her
as if she were a sack of garbage
here in this crossroad of empires.

Back in my hotel room I drink hot brandy
and read Graham Greene
while on CNN a new empire,
having neither the poetry and absolutism of the Turks,
nor the otherworldliness and willingness the Byzantines had
to cut out one's enemy's tongue in the name of God,
moves into the deserts of Mesopotamia.
A general with a Great Plains accent
stands in front of an easel and points out Baghdad and Damascus.
All he knows of these cities,
he learnt from a map in the back of his Bible.

Big Doors

for Andrew

I have seen with my own eyes doors so massive,
two men would have been required
to push open just one of them.
Bronze, grating over stone sills, or made of wood
from trees now nearly extinct.

Many things never to be seen again!
The fury of cavalry attacking at full gallop.
Little clouds of steam rising
from horse droppings
on most of the world's streets once.

Rooms amber with lamplight
perched above those streets.
Pilgrimage routes smoky with torchlight
from barony to principality through forests
which stood as a dark uncut authority.

A story that begins "Once upon a time".
Messengers, brigands, heralds
in a world unmapped from village to village.
Legends and dark misinformation,
graveyards crowded with ghosts.

And when the rider from that story at last arrives,
gates open at midnight to receive him.
Two men, two men we will never know,
lean into the effort of
pushing open each big door.

Snowflakes & a Jazz Waltz

for Barry Wallenstein

You have things to do, but the snow doesn't care.
As contemplation leads you
from window to window, the snow
accompanies you.
Whenever you glance up from the page, there it is—
layered, dense, constant.

It amplifies the volume of space
and gives you a way of telling time.

Eradication of emptiness, a specific against ennui,
it works, like truth, on a slant.

Its lightness
responds to gravity
by drift and evasion.
As you drive around town
it slackens and intensifies—
a sideways sizzle of dashes and dots.

While you circle the block, visualizing a parking place,
listening on tape to the cymbal-glide
and diminished chords of a jazz waltz
from forty years ago
when you were twenty,
a cash register rings

through the buzz and boozy hum of the Village Vanguard
one Sunday afternoon through cocktail chatter and
cigarette smoke exhaled
by people many of whom must now be dead.
Bill Evans is. Scott LaFaro is—
killed in a car crash
decades ago.

But not you. You drive
through the snow and the morning.
Snow drifts and ticks;
Bill Evans vamps,
and Scott LaFaro's fingers slap against the strings
of his standup bass
in time with the Honda's windshield wipers and
tyres whirring over packed snow.

It snows while you go into the bank and buy euros
and it's snowing when you
come out again.

Snowflakes—white constellations
dissolving.
                    Indelible
        snowflakes
printing the book of your hours.

As Long As I Have These Saddlebags

As long as I have these saddlebags
I think I will be all right.
The sun in their weave, their wool stained
        like a stained glass window,
their scorpion shapes and stylized camels
and cities with gates locked against marauders—
those clinched and vigilant symbols
doze like evolved watchdogs on my sofa.

One day I will lose this coin.
But as long as I have it,
I am walking the Street of the Fortunate
above the blue fabric, the silver scales of the sea—
through Cherries-that-Weigh-Down-the-Bough Street
on foot down the Street of the Little Holy Wisdom

keeping in my pocket the coin that will
        pay my way across
in a long wooden craft,
the boatman singing above the pulling oars.

My journeys
are slow marches
over mountains freckled with snow,
over black walnut trees that were cut down
to make my floors.

It's true I am kindling a fire today
on my own bricks,
not throwing together a rough blaze
with truck drivers and camel drivers and smugglers
stoking a water pipe on the dirt floor
of a caravansaray with gates standing open
to scavenger dogs gnawing bone-scraps, and wolves

and wind off the Hindu Kush.
I don't shiver with cold and the rain doesn't
needle my shoulders.
I don't have to favour my right knee as I climb
or wonder if my boots will fail me.

In the pilgrimage that is underway
I might not be among the trekkers.
But my fingers, like these saddlebags, are stained
        with the colours of the journey
and my hands smell of the currency of passage.
Praise God I am one of the travellers
as long as I have this coin in my pocket.

ACKNOWLEDGEMENTS

Grateful acknowledgement is made to Wesleyan University Press, publishers of *Sleep Watch* (first edition, 1969; second edition, 1983), *The Knife and Other Poems* (first printing, 1980; second printing, 1983), and *Our Flag Was Still There* (1984); to the University Press at Sewanee, Tennessee, publishers of *Sewanee in Ruins* (first edition, 1981; second edition, 1983); to David R. Godine, publishers of *The Stonecutter's Hand* (1995); to Salmon Publishing, publishers of *Today in the Café Trieste* (1997); to Story Line Press, publishers of *Six Mile Mountain* (2000); and to Copper Beech Press, publishers of *The New Life* (2008).

Thanks to Bow and Arrow Press in Cambridge, Massachusetts, who published "One Morning a Rose Blooms" as a broadside (2009); to North Carolina Wesleyan College, who published "Table" as a broadside (1997); to Palaemon Press in Winston-Salem, North Carolina, who published "Easter Week: Vermont" as a broadside (1982); to Pym-Randall Press in Cambridge, Massachusetts, who published "The Keeper" as a pamphlet (1968); and to White Creek Press in North Bennington, Vermont, for publishing part of "Fossils, Metal, & the Blue Limit" as a pamphlet (1982).

Thanks also to the editors of the following anthologies, compilations, and textbooks in which some of these poems have also appeared: *The Best of Irish Poetry*, edited by Maurice Riordan, Southword Editions, Cork (2007); *The Bread Loaf Anthology of Contemporary American Poetry*, University Press of New England (1985); *Cultural Horizons: A Festschrift in Honor of Talat S. Halman*, Syracuse University Press/Yapi Kredi Yayinlari, Istanbul (2001); *Family: A Celebration*, ed. Margaret Campbell, Princeton, NJ (1995); the *Harcourt Brace College Handbook of Creative Writing*, ed. Robert De Maria (1997); *Homewords: A Book of Tennessee Writers*, University of Tennessee Press, ed. Douglas Paschall (1996); *An Invitation to Poetry*, ed. Jay Parini, Prentice-Hall (1987); *The Made Thing, An Anthology of Contemporary Southern Poetry*, ed. Leon Stokesbury, University of Arkansas Press (1987 and 2000); *Mirrors, An Introduction to Literature*, ed. Knott and Reaske, Harper and Row (1988); *The Morrow Anthology of Younger American Poets*, Wm. Morrow & Co. (1985); *New American Poets of the 80s*, Wampeter Press (1984); *New Poems from the Third Coast: Contemporary Michigan Poetry*, ed. Delp, Hilberry & Kearns, Wayne State University Press (2000); *The Ploughshares Poetry Reader*, Ploughshares Press (1987); the *Poetry Book Society Anthology*, ed. Anne Stevenson (1991); *Poetry Daily Essentials*, Sourcebooks, Inc. (2007); *Poets of the New Century*, edited by Roger

Weingarten and Richard M. Higgerson, David R. Godine (2001); the *Southern California Anthology* (1993); *The Space Between Our Footsteps: Poems and Paintings from the Middle East*, selected by Naomi Shihab Nye (1998); *Ten American Poets*, ed. James Atlas, Carcanet Press, Cheshire, England (1974); *The Wesleyan Tradition: Four Decades of American Poetry*, Wesleyan/University Press of New England (1993); *A Year in Poetry*, ed. Thomas E. Foster & Elizabeth C. Guthrie, Crown Publishers, New York (1995).

Acknowledgement is made to Warner Brothers, Inc. for the right to publish four lines from "Just Like Tom Thumb's Blues", Music and Lyrics by Bob Dylan. Copyright (c) 1965.

Of the uncollected poems, "The Nest" first appeared in *The Southern Review*, "A House in the Country" in *Thumbscrew* and *Hunger Mountain*. "Once" first came out in *Five Points*. "Ars Poetica" was published in *Margie*.

Thanks to Grace Wells and to Alan Williamson for their help with some of these poems.